The Art and Science of Racehorse Training: the 'Bill' Marshall Guide

Introduction by

Jack Berry

Michael W. Marshall

LIST WORLD

Keepdate Publishing Ltd, 21 Portland Terrace, Newcastle upon Tyne, UK.

For Julie and Sylvie

Acknowledgements

I would like to thank the following for many useful discussions and their time spent reading draft manuscripts: Dr J W Reed, Respiration and Exercise Laboratory, University of Newcastle upon Tyne; Dr D J Marlin, Department of Physiology, The Animal Health Trust, Newmarket; and Jack Berry, Moss Side Racing Stables. I am especially grateful to Lucy Reece for her expert comments and stimulating ideas. Any errors are of course my own responsibility. Special thanks are due to Mrs R. Baker, Ms C. Dubois and Ms J. Hinves for their critical comments during the preparation of the book.
Cover photograph, preface photograph and plates 1, 2 & 3 © Chris Smith. All other photographs © M.W. Marshall.

Published by Keepdate Publishing Ltd
21 Portland Terrace, Jesmond,
Newcastle Upon Tyne NE2 1QQ.
Copyright Keepdate Publishing Ltd/M.W. Marshall, 1994
Cloth bound edition 1994 ISBN 0 9520494 X
Reprint 1997 ISBN 1 899506 40 3

Apart from any fair dealing for the purposes of research or private study, or criticism or review, as permitted under the Copyright, Designs and Patents Act 1988, this publication may not be reproduced, stored or transmitted, in any form or by any means, without the prior permission in writing of the publishers, or in the case of reprographic reproduction in accordance with the terms of licences issued by the Copyright Licensing Agency. Inquiries concerning reproduction outside those terms should be sent to the publishers at the address above.

Designed and typeset by Keepdate Publishing Ltd, Newcastle upon Tyne.
Printed and bound by Butler & Tanner Ltd, Somerset.

CONTENTS

Introduction	By Jack Berry	i
Preface		iii
Chapter 1	**Muscle Energetics: The Scientific Systems**	**1**
	The Muscular System	2
	Muscle Fuel: ATP and CP	3
	Energy Stores: Glycogen and Fat	4
	The Aerobic (Oxygen) Pathway	5
	The Anaerobic (No Oxygen) Pathway	7
	Muscle Fatigue	8
	The Aerobic and Anaerobic Pathways in Exercise	8
	Racehorse Fitness	10
Chapter 2	**Muscle & Movement**	**15**
	Slow Twitch (Type 1)	16
	Fast Twitch (Type 11)	16
	Type Depends on Electrical Activity	17
	Muscle Type Recruitment	18
	Blood Flow	18
	Heat Production and Loss	19
Chapter 3	**Three Important Systems**	**21**
	Hormonal System	21
	Circulatory System	23
	The Respiratory System	28
Chapter 4	**Racehorse Biomechanics**	**33**
	The Bones of the Skeleton	33
	The Moving Skeleton	35
	The Horse's Gait	39
	The Moving Horse	44
	The Resting Horse	49
	Conclusion	50
Chapter 5	**Stablecraft**	**51**
	Disease and Failure	52
	A Healthy Stable	54
	Tropical Stabling	59
	Grooming	60
	The Racehorse's Feet	62
Chapter 6	**Feeding to Win**	**67**
	Diet	67
	The Digestive System	68
	A Balanced Diet	69
	The Feed	71
	Water and Sweating	75

Chapter 7	**Buying & Breaking**	**79**
	The Sales	80
	Buying a Yearling	84
	Breaking In	86
Chapter 8	**Flat Race Training: the Routine**	**93**
	Tropical Routines	94
	Training in Temperate Climates	97
	The Lot System	99
	Evening Stables	104
	Travel and Routine	104
Chapter 9	**Training for the Jumps**	**107**
	Flat Racers as Jumpers	107
	The Jump Horses	108
	The Lot System	110
	Schooling a Jumper	111
	The Hurdle Stage	112
	The Steeplechaser	114
	Rest Days	115
Chapter 10	**Training to Win**	**117**
	Flat Racing	118
	Psychology of Training	119
	The Try Outs	122
	Fitness	125
	Jump Training	128
	The Weaker Horses	128
	Race Day Approaches	130
Chapter 11	**Entering & Travelling**	**133**
	The Entries	133
	Travelling	139
Chapter 12	**Race Day**	**143**
	Final Work Outs	144
	Saddling Up	145
	The Jockey - Trainer Relationship	147
	The Aftermath	152
Chapter 13	**Conformation & Condition**	**153**
	Conformation and Soundness	154
	Condition	159
Chapter 14	**Lameness: Assessment & Cure**	**163**
	The Search for Lameness	164
	The Neck and Back	166
	Forelimbs	167
	The Feet	173
	Hindlimb	174
	Muscle Lameness	176
Conclusion		**178**
Bibliography		**180**
Index		**181-184**

Introduction

One of the great fascinations of racing is that one never knows all the answers, never stops learning. I have always been a believer in the philosophy that, while one can have bad experiences - and we all have had plenty of those - there is no such thing as a bad experience; as Julius Caeser might have said, had he not been so concerned with conquering, "I came, I saw, I learnt".

It is hard to think of anyone in racing who has been more places, seen more sights - and thereby had more opportunity to learn than Bill Marshall. Of all the people whose racing brains one could have the opportunity of picking, his name must come very close to the top of the list. Bill has crammed more into his life than most certainly anyone else I know, and so I was delighted when I heard that he planned to share some of this experience with the rest of us.

As the title suggests, training is neither purely art nor science. The author brings Bill's understanding of the horse into play to show how the two parts inter-relate. We see exactly why the horse is not a machine, and benefit from the understanding of equine psychology which has come to Bill courtesy of the many horses which have passed through his hands. However, we also see that horses do have many similarities with machines, and in particular they are equally prone to failing which keeps mechanics in business the world over: machines break down! Just as a mechanic must have a total understanding of machines to fix them, so must the trainer be fully aware of the mechanics of the racehorse to realise what can go wrong, when something has gone wrong, what the exact problem is and how to cure it, and how to prevent it occurring again and exactly how, and more importantly, why the machine can be made to function more efficiently, ie how and why training makes a horse fitter.

The problem with any 'text book' about training racehorses is deciding what level of understanding its readers already have. Should one assume that one's readers are fairly expert already, and risk baffling the layman as one leaves certain basic topics untouched? Or should one cover all areas with meticulous thoroughness, and leave one's more learned readers feeling that they are being taught what they already know? Well, this book shows that this is not really an either/or situation, but that there is a third alternative: covering all areas, briefly but to the point, and moving swiftly and easily from the basic to the advanced, so that there will be clarity of understanding and interest for all, irrespective of what they do or do not know at the outset. Whether this book is read to learn new concepts, or to clarify the finer details, I am sure that the reader will find the study rewarding and enjoyable.

It does not surprise me that any book written with Bill's involvement would strike this happy balance. After all, he has never been an either/or person. He never had to agonise whether to train in Britain or overseas; whether to train in a large centre with everything laid on, or out in the country where one can run the set-up to suit oneself; whether to train flat horses or jumpers, sprinters or stayers - he has done the lot. Never mind training in the equine Metropolis of Newmarket and at Whitsbury, as fine a private training estate as one could find; never mind preparing *Raffingora* to break the world record down Epsom's five furlong track and sending jumpers to slog their way up the hill to the winners enclosure at Cheltenham - Bill has trained in four different continents!

To return to my original contention that one is never too old a dog to learn new tricks in this game, what I found particularly significant in the book was Bill's assertion that, even after all the years training in Australia, South Africa and so successfully in England, his learning process is still continuing with his stable in Barbados. If he is prepared to admit that he is still learning, I cannot see how the rest of us can turn our backs on as valuable a source of knowledge as this and I defy anyone to say, hand on heart, that reading this book has not been a worthwhile exercise.

Jack Berry,
Moss Side Racing Stables.

Preface

The crowd cheers as the sleek, muscular horses come flying down the final straight with their manes flying, their long thin legs pumping and their hooves barely touching the ground. The riding rhythm of the mud spattered jockeys accelerates as they frantically 'scrub' their mounts to the front. The noise from the stands rises as the horses struggle to outpace each other, reaching a roaring crescendo as the winning jockey passes the post.

The roar subsides, the triumphant jockey slows his mount, pats its neck, whispers a few words into its ear before raising an arm to acknowledge the scattered applause and the excited cries from the punters who backed a winner, or the delighted shouts of "well done" from the owner. Then it's off to the winners' enclosure for unsaddling while the lucky punters, owners and friends celebrate with champagne.

Horse Racing - the images conjured up by those two words are numerous, exciting and glamorous. To name a few: the photo finishes; Ascot; the Grand National; grey toppers; the Queen; top jockeys, Fred Archer, Sir Gordon Richards, Arthur 'Scobie' Breasley, Lester Piggott,

Pat Eddery, Fred Winter, Tim Maloney, John Francome, Peter Scudamore and many more; top trainers, Noel Murless, George Todd, Jack Jarvis, Vincent O'Brien, Jack Berry and the rest; rich owners; millionaires; bookmakers; betting syndicates; great and brave horses and the thousands of unsung heroes; the flutter on the Derby; champagne; and the scuffed, torn betting slips blowing in the wind in the main stand after everyone has gone home.

Horse racing is a long established part of the British way of life and, as a spectacle, enjoyed by every stratum of society. But behind all the excitement and glamour of each race, there is a small army of dedicated people bringing these finely tuned thoroughbreds to a state of readiness. In Britain, for example, there are tens of thousands of people working daily with racehorses to try and produce winners or to make a day at the races an enjoyable event: the grooms, the work riders, the jockeys, the horse transporters, the head lads, the vets, the blacksmiths, the track officials, the caterers, and many others, including the trainer.

The racehorse trainer has a difficult and multifaceted job with the ultimate aim of making the horses under his control run faster than any other horse over a given distance. The trainer is always judged by results and without winners soon lapses into obscurity with owners withdrawing their horses to place them in other trainers' yards.

The aim of this book is to describe both the art and science of racehorse training and the problems and difficulties facing a trainer in the intensely competitive world of the race track. Much of the practical material comes from a racehorse trainer, the writer's father Bill Marshall, who uses both art and science in plying his skills.

It is possible to train by the so called 'make or break' system whereby each year a trainer and his owners purchase substantial numbers of well-bred thoroughbreds. All these horses are subjected to a similar and rigorous basic training programme and those that 'break down' or are not fast enough in speed trials are rejected. Today this approach is practised by very few trainers as it requires an enormous annual capital outlay to purchase high quality horses as well as extensive funds to run a large racing stable and pay the staff: costs which have to be met even when the yard is not producing winners.

The make or break system can be effective but it is costly and inefficient. Nowadays nearly all successful trainers 'custom train', whereby each horse is taken through an exercise programme that is designed to obtain the best possible performance on race day. A single trainer will usually train around 40 horses as custom training is very time consuming and trainers working more than 40 racehorses will usually need to employ an under-trainer.

Thirty years ago the trainer relied more on the art of training than the science. Some of his 'art' (unlike today there were almost no successful female trainers) was the trainer's intuitive use of today's recently discovered scientific methods of sports' training and exercise physiology. Currently, training is more rationalised and scientific owing to these recent, rapid advances in medical, sport and veterinary sciences. Equine functional anatomy, human and equine physiology and the science of horse management and veterinary practice have all seen major advances in the last few decades and the rate of progress does not appear to be slowing. But successful racehorse training is not a science. The art of training has played and will continue to play a vital role - sound stable craft, superb horsemanship, experience and horse psychology are all subjects that cannot be studied, or are difficult to study, in the laboratory.

The dividing line between art and science is never clear. All trainers take into account, when devising their exercise regimes, the breeding and the 'nature' of a horse: two extremely important factors which affect athletic ability and each is both an art and a science. The breeding of a winning racehorse is, despite an enormous amount of scientific research, still very much an art and the old maxim 'put the best with the best and hope for the best' continues to apply. The horse's nature, or psychological make-up, is very important in winning races. Many modern day trainers believe that great racehorses love to race, love to win and hate to be beaten.

Racehorse training is a difficult way of life: the trainer is tied to the animals night and day, year in and year out. The trainer is dependent on the owners for supplying the horses; dependent on the new 'kings of racing', the multi-million-pound-earning top jockeys, and the trainer.

requires that everyone in the racing stables works together as a team. On race day the horse may be in the right race, in perfect physical and mental shape but the trainer may be simply unlucky, and through no fault of jockey or trainer, the horse fails to win.

To be a trainer you have to love horses, want to spend your time with them and to learn to roll with the punches. "I've been around horses for almost all my life", says Bill Marshall. "I had my first horse, *Bobby*, when I was five years old and rode him bare back with a head collar. I was riding racehorses when I was 12 or 13 years old as my father always had a few in training. When I was 14 years old I ran away to sea and joined a tramp ship as a 'deckie' because I wanted to be a jockey and my father wouldn't have it. I jumped ship in Australia and started riding and training there. I went from there to South Africa where I worked as a rigger in a mine and continued to ride and train racehorses. I was doing well there and flew home in my private plane at the outbreak of the Second World War to enlist in the RAF. After the war I continued to ride and started training in earnest, obtaining my licence to train in the early 1950s.

"As a trainer I seem to have spent half my life looking after muscles, ligaments and tendons. It is good to pass on some of the knowledge and experience I've gained to younger trainers, and to those people, and there are an awful lot of them, who are interested in horse racing and training. No doubt most other trainers have many good ideas of their own and I've learnt a lot from other people's experiences. One thing I have noticed is that all great trainers have a special relationship with animals, a sort of sixth sense - the horses like you and you like them."

Bill Marshall has trained racehorses for over 60 years in temperate and more recently tropical climates and believes now, in his late seventies, that he is a better trainer than he was when he left Newmarket, England in the 1980s. There he had superb amenities: canters, gallops, grooms, work riders and jockeys. But in the Caribbean where the conditions are less than perfect his racehorses are just as fit and successful as when they were trained at Newmarket. Racehorses are fragile animals but they have proved to be a lot tougher than he once thought. In the

Caribbean their legs are subject to a lot of stress. The race track is either baked rock-hard by the tropical sun or a soft, sticky quagmire because of tropical downpours. He trains on heavy sand tracks and his gallops are hard dirt tracks. Yet, incredibly, after months of almost continuous training and racing the horses' legs remain sound. Thus even after years of experience the successful trainer continues to learn.

Successful trainers win races by reducing the element of risk on the race track. They use both Art and Science. The first chapters of this book describe many recent scientific advances and their significance in custom training. A large part of the book deals with the trainer's art: intuition, sensitivity and a 'feeling for animals' are as important today as they ever were.

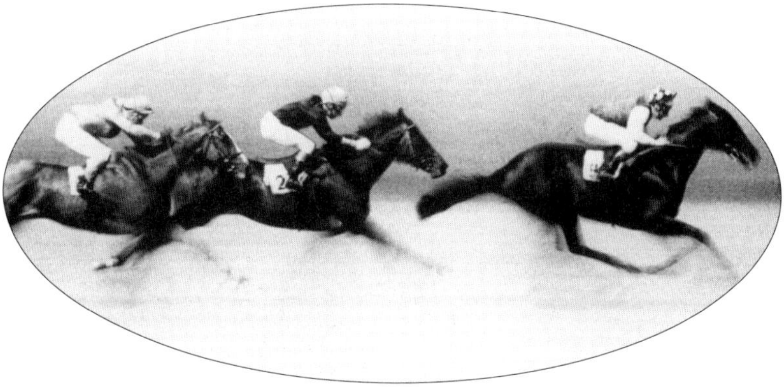

CHAPTER ONE

Muscle Energetics

The Scientific Systems

A racehorse is a highly evolved animal - a vertebrate and a mammal. Animals, like non-living materials, obey the laws of physics and chemistry so a scientific approach to the training of racehorses involves a scientific understanding of how the horse's body functions.

It is possible to consider the bodily functions being composed of separate systems: the nervous system, the digestive–energy producing system, the hormonal system and so on. But the functioning of one system cannot be viewed in isolation since the bodily activities are intimately dependent on one another. For instance the way in which oxygen, an essential ingredient for muscle contraction, is supplied to working muscles will depend, amongst other things, upon: the racehorse's general fitness; the state of the heart and lungs, which respectively drive the blood round the body and supply the blood with oxygen; the elasticity of the blood vessels (arteries, veins and capillaries) and the chemical make-up of the blood; the source of energy; the nervous system which, amongst many other things, controls heart beat and respiration rate; the horse's psychological state and the chemical changes that occur within the muscles as the horse exercises.

Although the interdependence of all the racehorse's different systems should never be forgotten, a racehorse trainer is mainly concerned with developing the muscular system to its full potential, for it is the muscles - the skeletal muscles - that drive the limbs of the running horse. But the trainer cannot develop the strength and efficiency of the muscular system in isolation. There must be a parallel development of the racehorse's skeletal system, its cardiopulmonary system (the heart and lungs) and its digestive–energy producing system to supply the fuel for muscle contraction.

The Muscular System

The horse's muscular system performs a variety of different functions. Muscles are not only responsible for the tremendous driving power of the horse's hind limbs, they are also, for example, responsible for the beating of the heart, the contracting and dilating of the pupil of the eye and the movement of food along the bowel.

In mammals there are basically three types of muscle: skeletal muscle which, as its name implies, is responsible for the movement of the skeleton; cardiac muscle for the beating of the heart; and smooth muscle which is responsible, for example, for the changes in diameter of the pupil or for the movement of food along the intestine.

Muscles can be thought of as biological machines that convert energy that is ultimately derived from the horse's food into mechanical work. Muscles only carry out work in one way and that is by shortening (contracting). They make up about one third of the body weight of racehorses, which have more muscle bulk and less fat than other horse breeds.

Skeletal Muscle

Racehorses also have more skeletal muscle than most other horses and their speed is almost directly related to the work done by the hind legs. There is almost four times as much skeletal muscle in the hind limbs as compared to the forelimbs.

Each skeletal muscle is attached to the racehorse's skeleton at each end by a non-elastic, fibrous tissue - the tendon. Each muscle has an artery and a vein. The artery brings in oxygen which is used to burn up energy stores (sugars and fats, see below) to release energy for the contraction process. The vein takes away the waste products (mainly carbon dioxide, water and lactic acid, see below) of the chemical reactions associated with this process. The muscle also receives a nerve so that the contraction can be regulated by signals travelling to it from the brain and spinal cord. There are even special organs in the tendons that send back information to the brain about the length of the muscle and the tension in the tendons. The blood vessels, nerves and muscles are collectively known as muscle tissue.

The body of a muscle is composed of fibres, long thin animal 'cells', sometimes metres long, that have specially evolved to convert stored chemical energy into contractile force. The basic building block of all animals is the cell. In complex animals, cells are highly modified to perform different functions and muscle (and nerve) cells are some of the most specialised of all animal cells.

Force of Contraction

Each skeletal muscle fibre receives a single nerve fibre that is responsible for the 'switching on' of muscle fibre contraction. *The force of a muscle contraction depends on the frequency of the nervous activity and on the thickness of the muscle.* The higher the rate of electrical activity, up to a maximum level, the greater the force of the contraction. Also the larger the muscle fibre diameter, the greater is the force of contraction.

Muscle Fuel: ATP and CP

All muscle contractions require a source of fuel or energy as well as a supply of oxygen to 'burn up' the fuel. In all biological systems immediately available energy is stored in special substances or energy–giving 'molecules' which have energy 'locked into' the bonds between the atoms that make up these molecules. Onset of muscular contraction is brought about by the release of this locked–in energy to the muscle cell's chemical machinery that causes contraction.

ATP

An extremely important energy-giving molecule in racehorses is Adenosine Triphosphate (ATP). This is the primary molecule that drives the 'contractile machinery' of the racehorse's muscle cells. The contractile machinery is a series of long complex molecules situated inside each muscle fibre. In the presence of ATP, the long molecules shorten by actually 'racking' alongside each other thus causing the muscle fibre to shorten or 'contract'. A single muscle contraction is known as a twitch.

ATP is found in the fluid that makes up the bulk (or the 'intracellular contents') of a muscle fibre and it is estimated that there are only enough ATP molecules in each equine muscle fibre for some ten twitches before it is all used up. Once the intracellular stores of ATP are used up muscle fibres become very stiff and the muscle no longer responds to nerve or electrical stimulation and enters into a state known as 'rigor'. The stiffening of the muscles of a mammalian corpse (rigor mortis) is the direct result of ATP depletion!

CP

Another important energy giving substance or molecule is energised Creatine Phosphate or CP which also plays an important role in driving the contractile machinery of the muscle cells. CP is also present inside the cell and its role is to quickly 'recharge' the ATP after the ATP is broken down in delivering energy to the muscle cell's contractile machinery. This re–energising process of ATP by CP continues as the muscle is actively contracting. However there is a limited supply of CP in equine skeletal muscle and it has been estimated that after about some 100 contractions this energy source would be used up.

Energy Stores: Glycogen and Fat

The contracting muscle thus has to obtain energy by another means and it uses two sources: sugars or fats. Energy stored in the ATP molecules (that can be thought of as the muscle's fuel) is obtained, or as the bichemists say 'synthesised', from the chemical breakdown of sugars and fats.

Sugars are a class of water–soluble carbohydrates and one important sugar used by the racehorse to obtain energy is 'glucose'. Glucose comes from stores of 'animal starch' or 'glycogen' that is stored in muscle fibres (and also in the liver) as minute undissolved granules. Long chains of glucose molecules are bonded together to form glycogen and 'enzymes' break down these long molecular chains to give glucose molecules.

The other energy source comes from substances known as 'fatty acids' and these come from the racehorse's fat stores. Most racehorses in training are sleek and muscular and only have a very limited amount of stored fat. However, although stored fat is extra weight to carry for the racehorse and fat restricts heat loss during exercise, it is still an important energy store. Fatty acids and glucose are found dissolved in the fluid that is inside the muscle fibres and they are also carried from other reservoirs to the muscle in the blood stream. Without the breakdown of sugars and fats to form ATP the muscles would run out of energy and stop contracting.

The chemical breakdown of fatty acids, glycogen and glucose to give the energy that is carried in the ATP molecules can take place in the presence or absence of oxygen.

The Aerobic (Oxygen) Pathway

The formation of energy rich ATP by a series of chemical reactions that occur in the presence of oxygen is known as the Aerobic (oxygen) Pathway and takes place in specialised parts of the muscle cells (and in all mammalian cells) that are known as the 'mitochondria'. The mitochondria are microscopic particles and can be thought of as the 'power stations' of the cells.

When racehorses are undergoing steady, light to moderate exercise and the muscle cells are being well supplied with oxygen the Aerobic Pathway's formation of ATP is the main way in which energy is supplied to drive the muscle's contractile machinery.

Although the break down of glycogen and glucose in the presence of oxygen results in the production of large amounts of ATP (to be precise 36 molecules of ATP per molecule of glucose), it takes the racehorse time, a few minutes, for the chemical pathways to be switched on so as to reach these optimum levels of ATP production. However once switched on and providing there is a plentiful supply of oxygen this is the most efficient pathway for energy production.

Aerobic Conditions
'Aerobic conditions' of exercise are when oxygen is readily available to the equine muscle cells as in light to moderate exercise. Under these conditions the production of ATP by the Aerobic Pathway in the muscle fibres results in the formation of carbon dioxide and water. These are the so-called 'waste products' that result from the 'burning up' of the fuel which provides ATP and brings about muscle contraction. The carbon dioxide and water is readily removed from the body at the lungs when the racehorse breathes out.

Fatty acids from the horse's fat reserves also produce ATP using the same biochemical (mitochondrial) mechanisms for energy production as when glycogen is broken down. Fatty acids are also broken down to carbon dioxide and water when they produce ATP.

The longer the length of time the Aerobic Pathway is in operation as the main energy producing pathway in a race the greater the energy available to the horse. As the racehorse enters more deeply into its training programme the training regime increases both the number and the size of the mitochondria in muscle fibres. There is also an increase in the chemicals associated with the production of ATP by the Aerobic Pathway which must therefore improve the overall efficiency of energy production for muscle contraction by this pathway.

Steady Exercise
Steady work training for racehorses appears to shift the fuel usage of the Aerobic Pathway from glycogen granules to fatty acids. Thus a training programme that consists of long steady exercise reduces fat reserves more readily than one which consists of bursts of activity.

Severe Exercise
During heavy or severe exercise it has been shown that a racehorse's

muscles are being poorly supplied with oxygen. It is thought that this oxygen lack in exercise is partly due to the inability of the lungs, heart and the blood to deliver oxygen at a sufficient rate. The energy/ATP production for muscle contraction is then predominantly by another chemical pathway that is known as the Anaerobic (no oxygen) Pathway.

The Anaerobic (No Oxygen) Pathway

In severe exercise a thoroughbred's skeletal muscles do not receive the same amounts of oxygen as when they are undergoing light to moderate exercise. As a result there is a shortage of oxygen, an 'oxygen lack', for energy production for muscle contraction (ie ATP formation) by the Aerobic Pathway. It has been shown that under these conditions of oxygen lack the muscle cells switch the mechanism for energy production/ATP formation for contraction to the so-called 'oxygen lack' or Anaerobic Pathway.

The 'waste product' of the series of chemical reactions in the Anaerobic Pathway is lactic acid and not, as in the Aerobic Pathway, carbon dioxide and water. Lactic acid is more difficult to remove from the blood stream than carbon dioxide and water, and with continued oxygen shortage the lactic acid concentration increases until it builds to such levels that it is thought by many (but not all) exercise scientists to reach sufficiently high levels as to actually inhibit the contractile mechanisms (see muscle fatigue page 8).

The Anaerobic Pathway is less efficient at producing energy for muscle contraction than the Aerobic Pathway. This can be measured scientifically as the amount of ATP produced from a molecule of glucose (one molecule of glucose is broken down to produce only three molecules of ATP in the Anaerobic Pathway compared to 36 for each molecule of glucose in the Aerobic Pathway). However ATP production by the Anaerobic Pathway does have the advantage over the Aerobic Pathway in that this Anaerobic Pathway is switched on more rapidly at the onset of exercise.

One source (Swann) estimates that during the first 10 seconds of a race 85% of energy production is by the Anaerobic Pathway, the Aerobic Pathway supplying only 15%. However if maximum effort is continued for two minutes the Aerobic Pathway supplies 50% of the energy production and this increases to 70% by four minutes.

Muscle Fatigue

There are large stores of glycogen in the racehorse's muscles and liver. Stored fat makes up some five per cent of the total body weight of the racehorse. Together these glycogen and fat stores are sufficient to produce enough ATP for thousands of muscle fibre contractions.

As a general rule when exercise severity is increased beyond a certain level it is not the fuel supply that becomes the limiting factor to muscle contraction but oxygen lack and then the contracting muscles suffer from 'muscle fatigue'.

It has been suggested above, that inhibition of muscle contraction, i.e. 'muscle fatigue', is directly related to lactic acid production when the oxygen supply to the contracting muscles becomes a limiting factor and lactic acid is produced in significant quantities by the Anaerobic Pathway.

However not all exercise physiologists believe that muscle fatigue in severe exercise is directly related to the increase in lactic acid production. Other possibilities exist such as a gradual fall in ATP concentration or even, as has been recently suggested, a rise in potassium that passes from inside to outside the muscles and in a complicated way makes the muscle cells 'less excitable'.

But most exercise scientists do believe that: *high intensity training of a racehorse (fast work) causes an enhancement of the Anaerobic Pathway and thus an improved efficiency of energy production from energy stores (ie glycogen).*

The Aerobic and Anaerobic Pathways in Exercise

It is now believed that in moderate exercise, such as in a slow canter, probably both Anaerobic and Aerobic Pathways are used to generate ATP for muscle contraction. The Anaerobic process produces ATP at the beginning of the exercise period and the Aerobic Pathway switches in after a few minutes to predominate towards the end of the exercise period.

The Energy Production Pathways

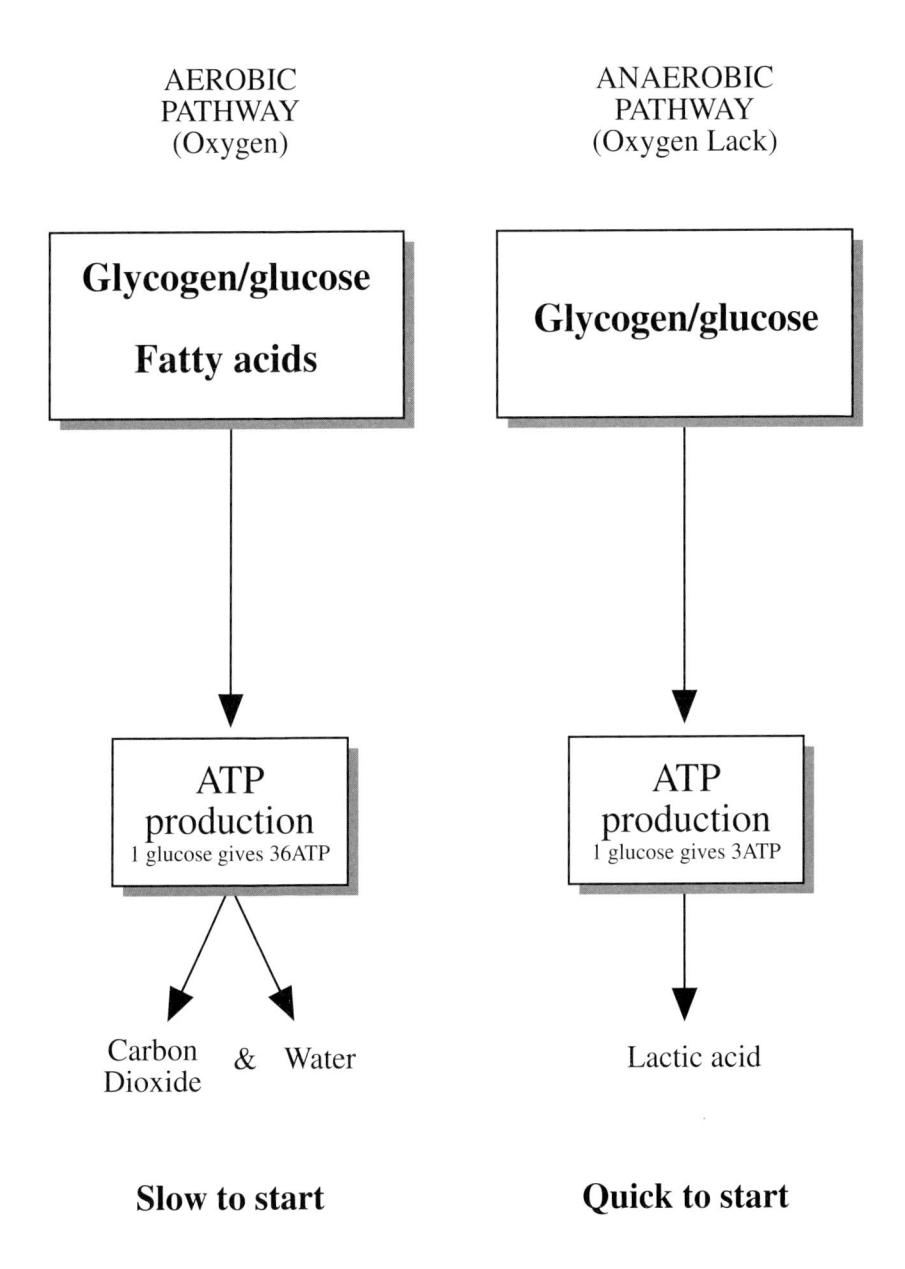

AEROBIC PATHWAY (Oxygen)	ANAEROBIC PATHWAY (Oxygen Lack)
Glycogen/glucose **Fatty acids**	**Glycogen/glucose**
↓	↓
ATP production 1 glucose gives 36ATP	ATP production 1 glucose gives 3ATP
↓	↓
Carbon Dioxide & Water	Lactic acid
Slow to start	**Quick to start**

Warm Up

At the start of any form of exercise energy/ATP production for skeletal muscle contraction is probably by the Anaerobic Pathway. If the exercise regime is only moderate it still takes a few minutes following the onset of exercise before the amount of ATP produced to sustain even a moderate level of exercise can be formed. This time lag probably occurs because it takes time to mobilise the glycogen and fatty acid stores and fully switch on the chemical mechanism associated with the Aerobic Pathway.

From this it would appear that for a long steady race a racehorse should be 'warmed up' to get over the anaerobic period of ATP production and switch energy production to the more energy-efficient Aerobic Pathway.

There is thus a sound scientific basis for dividing exercise into Aerobic exercise (moderate sustained exercise) and Anaerobic exercise (intense, short term bursts of work). Racehorses are generally classified as sprinters or stayers and thus sprinters should have well developed Anaerobic Pathways, stayers Aerobic Pathways.

Racehorse Fitness

Lactic acid, the end waste-product of the Anaerobic Pathway, has to be broken down by the racehorse's metabolism. This is in contrast to the waste-products of the Aerobic Pathway, carbon dioxide and water, which are expired by the horse's lungs. One scientific way of measuring the 'fitness' of a racehorse is measuring the speed in which the lactate concentration *increases* in its bloodstream following the onset of exercise. That is the longer the lactic acid takes to build up at a given work rate the *fitter* the horse.

The ability of the blood stream to deal with any increase in acid is known as the 'buffering capacity'. If the acid is mopped up by circulating 'buffering substances' in the blood then the proposed harmful effects of lactic acid build up can, to some extent, be counteracted.

It has been shown that high intensity (anaerobic) training increases the buffering capacity of the racehorse's blood which means that a trained racehorse's muscles are less susceptible to fatigue.

Warming up before the start.

The Oxygen Debt

It has also been suggested that the 'fitness' of a racehorse can be quantified by the speed at which the lactic acid concentration is *reduced* in the blood stream.

Lactic acid breakdown requires oxygen. And during a post exercise period the racehorse is said to be in 'oxygen debt' (to its muscles) since extra oxygen is required to breakdown the lactic acid. This oxygen debt is measured post exercise, and is the extra amount of oxygen taken up when compared to the pre-exercise period.

The experiments that showed racehorses had an oxygen debt were conducted in laboratories where racehorses were exercised under controlled conditions on treadmills. Sophisticated instruments were attached to the horse for measuring the oxygen uptake from the lungs and analysing the respiratory gases in the animal's blood. It was found that the degree of the oxygen debt depended upon the severity of the exercise - the greater the work performed by the horse the greater the debt.

| CHAPTER ONE | *The Art & Science of Racehorse Training* |

Even after light exercise where there is no lactic acid to break down there is a slight oxygen debt due, it is thought, to a requirement for oxygen to refurbish used ATP stores in the muscle and also to replace oxygen in the special carrier molecules (myoglobin) that exist to facilitate the transport of oxygen from the blood to the muscles. Following severe exercise the oxygen of the oxygen debt must also be used to replace myoglobin oxygen and rebuild ATP, as well as breaking down lactic acid and rebuilding glucose and glycogen stores.

Training racehorses reduces the magnitude of the 'oxygen debt' and increases the speed/ability with which the stores of glycogen and fat (the muscle fibres' energy stores) in the liver and the muscle fibres are rebuilt after exercise.

Warm Down

One important scientific finding that has come out of studies on oxygen debt and lactic acid breakdown is that lactic acid removal by chemical pathways is much aided by a mild exercise and that a 'warm down' after heavy bouts of training or racing is most beneficial. It has been shown that an active warm down exercise, which might be as little as a fast walk or a slow trot, can almost double the rate of lactic acid removal following exercise.

'Fitness' is thus dramatically improved by a small bout of post-exercise exercise (warm-down) if fitness is measured as the speed with which lactic acid is removed from the blood stream. The greater the speed of removal the greater the fitness.

Fitness and the Skill Factor

The conversion of stored fuel such as glycogen and fat to bring about the muscle fibre contraction and the effects of training on the Aerobic and Anaerobic Pathways have been discussed in some detail.

It is also likely that training improves the efficiency of the skeletal muscle motor by 'learning' as the racehorse learns how to fine tune and control its skeletal muscles. This learning corresponds to the 'skill factor' in human athletes. For example a trained racehorse will automatically adjust its leading, respond to the jockey's command to accelerate or hold back by controlling its stride length and frequency - all extremely important factors if the most efficient use is to be obtained out of the precious supplies of muscle fuel. Thus indirectly the skill factor has a bearing on muscle fitness and energetics.

Thus from a relatively simplistic study of equine muscle energetics it can be seen that there are a number of very important pre and post exercise practices when training racehorses that have a sound scientific basis.

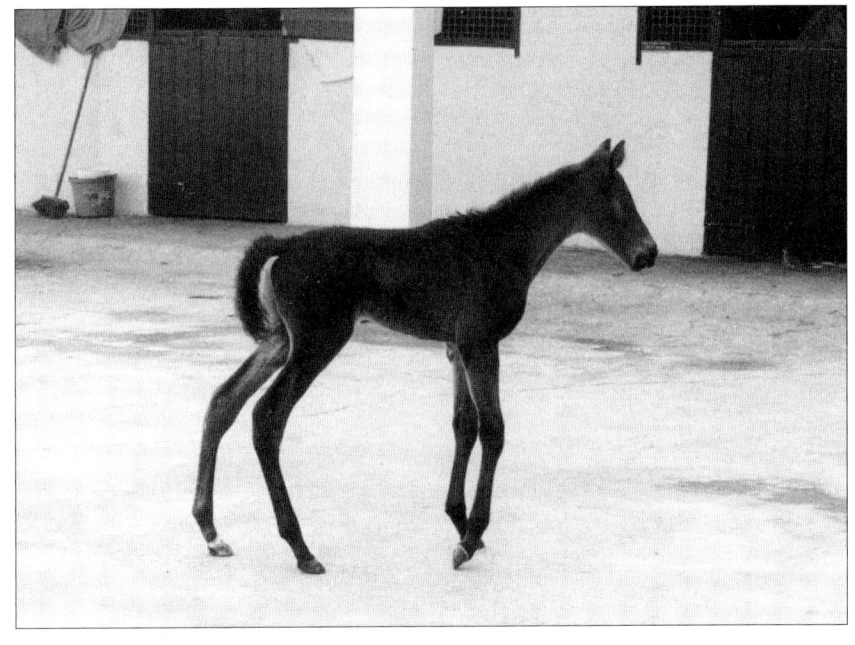

From small beginnings grow great racehorses.

CHAPTER ONE │ *The Art & Science of Racehorse Training*

'Bill' Marshall, National Hunt jockey.

'Bill' Marshall, National Hunt Trainer.

CHAPTER TWO

Muscle and Movement

Chapter One showed how the energy production aspect of racehorse skeletal muscle contraction was important in a racing and training programme. In this chapter the characteristics of racehorse skeletal muscle contraction are examined in more detail.

The body of a skeletal muscle is composed of large numbers of parallel running muscle cells or *fibres*, each fibre about the thickness of a human hair. Three main *types* of skeletal muscle fibre have been described in racehorse skeletal muscle, Type I, Type IIA and Type IIB, and each of the three types has a characteristic structure and function.

Racehorse skeletal muscle can be functionally divided into two classes - slow or fast twitch muscle - a division that is based upon differences in the speed with which the muscles contract and in the ability of the muscles to resist fatigue. This classification depends on the relative proportions of the three muscle fibre *types* within each muscle body. Slow twitch muscles are mainly Type I muscle fibres while fast twitch muscles are predominantly Type IIA and B fibres.

It is important that a racehorse trainer has an understanding of these three skeletal muscle types as much of the horses's athletic ability depends on the development and distribution of the three different muscle types within the body of a racehorse's skeletal muscle. Racehorses can also be broadly classified into two groups, stayers or sprinters, and the relative proportions of slow and fast twitch skeletal muscle will affect the racehorse's classification and its performance.

Slow Twitch (Type I)

Slow twitch muscles, sometimes known as Type I muscles, take longer to contract and are more resistant to fatigue than fast twitch or Type II muscles. Slow twitch muscles are best adapted for long term muscle activity - for example the postural muscles. Slow twitch or Type I muscle fibres have a chemical system that readily utilises the Aerobic Pathway to produce ATP (see Chapter 1).

Fast Twitch (Type II)

Fast twitch or Type II muscles contract faster than Type I fibres but they fatigue more quickly and are thus best adapted for short term phasic muscle activity. The muscle fibres use the Anaerobic Pathway more readily than slow twitch fibres to form ATP for muscle contraction.

From this it would appear that sprinters should have more fast twitch type (anaerobic) muscle fibres than slow twitch (aerobic) muscle fibres. There is some evidence based on the difference between horse breeds to suggest that this is the case.

Fast twitch, Type II, skeletal muscle fibres are usually further subdivided into two groups: Type IIA and Type IIB.

Type IIA and IIB Fibres

Although Type IIA fibres are classified as fast twitch fibres they have many of the characteristics of Type I slow twitch muscle fibres. The ability of Type I slow twitch muscle fibres to produce large amounts of ATP aerobically is also, perhaps surprisingly, an important physiological feature of Type IIA fast twitch fibres.

Muscles made up of Type IIA and Type I fibres are also similar in that they appear more red in colour when compared to muscles composed mainly of Type IIB fibres. Thus slow twitch muscles are sometimes called 'red muscles' and fast twitch muscles are sometimes known as 'white muscles'. This is due to the larger number of small blood vessels (the capillaries) that carry the blood to the muscles from the arteries in slow twitch muscles. The 'redness' in Type I and Type IIA muscles is also partly due to the presence of a special molecule (myoglobin) that is thought to improve the speed at which oxygen reaches the working muscles from the blood.

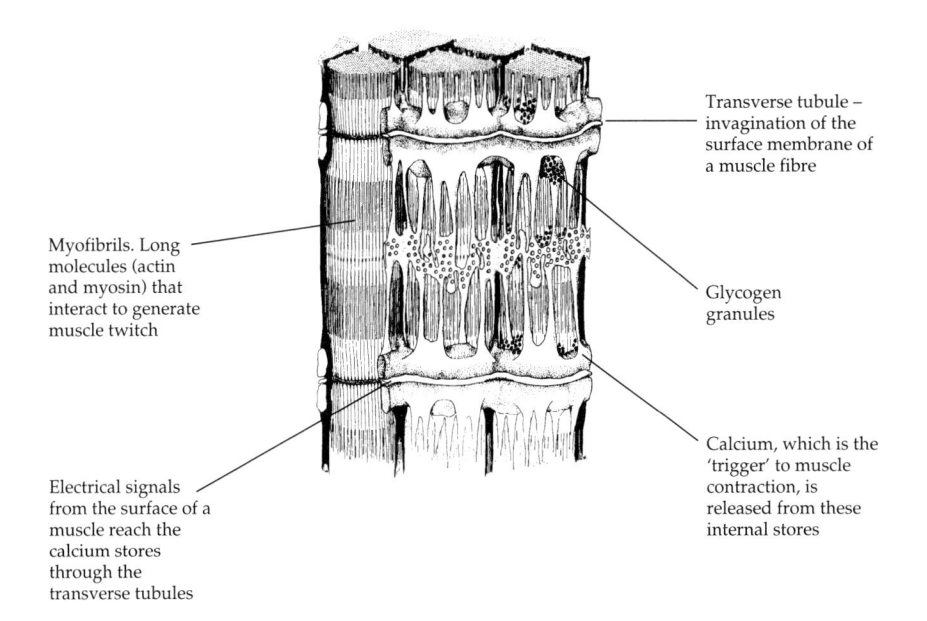

Inside a skeletal muscle fibre (after Peachey).

It is useful to think of Type IIA muscle fibres in terms of their structure and function as being intermediary between Type I & Type IIB muscle fibres.

Type Depends on Electrical Activity

In the skeletal muscles of a racehorse most muscle fibres (around 80%) are fast twitch Type II fibres. There is recent scientific evidence that suggests that the classification of muscle fibre types into fast and slow is dependent upon the pattern of electrical activity that the muscles receive from the nerve that supplies each muscle fibre. Slow Type I fibres have smaller diameter nerves than Type II fibres and receive a steady supply of low frequency electrical stimulation from the nerves.

Type Transformation and Training

It is now well established from studies involving direct sampling of racehorse skeletal muscles (biopsies) that long steady work outs convert Type IIB (sprint) fibres into Type IIA (sprint/endurance) fibres.

There is also some evidence that following similar training - long, steady work outs - Type IIA fast twitch muscle fibres will transform to

Type I, slow twitch, endurance. This transformation of Type IIB to IIA (and Type IIA to I) fibres following steady work training is probably due to the low frequency pattern of nervous activity that the muscles receive during the training period.

The opposite conversion of Type I slow to Type II fast twitch fibres is said to be more difficult to achieve in training probably because most of the time, even when involved in an intensive training programme, the racehorse is not exercising and the muscles are receiving only low frequency nervous stimulation when the horse is stabled.

Muscle Type Recruitment

An important aspect of the development of power from a muscle during exercise is the way in which the muscle fibres are switched on or 'recruited'. Slow twitch, Type I muscle fibres are recruited first in light to moderate work. This is because they have smaller diameter nerve fibres which have a lower 'threshold' to electrical stimulation from the central nervous system than the larger diameter nerve fibres of the Type II fast twitch muscle fibres. As these slow twitch fibres switch on in low to moderate forms of exercise they will obtain energy for their contractions from both the Anaerobic and Aerobic Pathways. If exercise is kept to a moderate level they will, after a few minutes, produce large quantities of energy giving ATP molecules by the Aerobic Pathway (see Chapter 1).

Type II fibres will be switched on as the exercise level is increased. Because of their smaller size Type IIA fibres will be switched on before Type IIB fibres. Type IIB fibres are less able to use the Aerobic Pathway and are the least fatigue resistant of the three muscle types. As exercise levels approach maximum, oxygen will increasingly be in short supply. Type IIA & IIB fibres will produce lactic acid by the Anaerobic Pathway and the muscle will fatigue (see pages 8-9).

Blood Flow

Type I and Type IIA muscles have more muscle capillaries than Type IIB muscles. Muscle capillaries are minute blood vessels found close to the muscle fibres and it is the capillaries that deliver oxygenated blood and nutrients to the muscles and remove the waste products of muscle contraction such as carbon dioxide, water and lactic acid.

It is now established that long-term exercise will increase the number of capillaries (muscle capillary density) that supply any racehorse muscle. An increase in the number of blood vessels supplying a muscle means that there will be an increase in the blood flow to the muscle. An increase in blood flow to and from the muscle means that more oxygen can be supplied to a working muscle and the waste products of exercise are more readily removed. Increased capillarisation thus helps reduce the recovery period and muscle fatigue.

Heat Production and Loss

Heat build up during exercise can become a serious problem, especially in the tropics as excessive heat production will damage and eventually destroy muscle. Heat is generated when ATP (see Chapter 1) breaks down during the process of muscle contraction. The process of releasing energy locked in the ATP (and CP) molecules to the muscle's contractile machinery is extremely wasteful - some 75% of the energy that is locked into the ATP molecule being lost as heat. Likewise the reformation of ATP is inefficient, involving significant heat loss.

Heat is removed from exercising racehorse muscles by the blood and the greater the blood flow through a muscle the better the heat removal. Heat is eventually lost from the racehorse through the lungs and skin. Respiration is responsible for a small heat loss when cold air enters the lungs and is heated by the blood. But most heat is lost through the skin either by convection, when the outside temperature is lower than that of the horse, or by the evaporation of sweat which causes the temperature of the skin to drop. The greater the blood flow through the skin the more efficient is heat loss by convection and evaporation. Thus the increased number of capillaries that occurs as a result of long term exercise will also improve the efficiency of heat loss in the trained racehorse.

The anatomical and functional differences in skeletal muscle fibre discussed in this chapter are best summarised as a Table:

Table 1: Racehorse Skeletal Muscle Fibre Types.

Features	Type I	Type IIA	Type IIB
Twitch	Slow	Fast	Fastest
Muscle Diameter	Moderate	Small	Large
Nerve Diameter	Small	Medium	Large
Recruited (activated)	First	Second	Third
Colour	Red	Red	White
Myoglobin	High	High	Low
Capillary Density	High	High	Moderate
Glycogen Conc.	Similar	Similar	Similar
Lactic Acid Production	Moderate	High	High
Aerobic Activity	High	High	Low
Anaerobic Activity	Low	High	High

CHAPTER THREE

Three Important Systems

The racehorse's muscular system has been examined to show how it produces movement by burning of a sugar and fat fuel and how custom training affects this system. But the muscular system does not act in isolation; other biological systems like the horse's hormonal, circulatory and respiratory systems, while often acting at a distance, have important effects on skeletal muscle contraction. All three systems have profound effects on the health, fitness and performance of a racehorse and a modern day racehorse trainer has to have, at a minimum, a working knowledge of the inter–dependence of these systems and how their inter–relationships are affected by training.

Hormonal System

Hormones are the chemical messengers of the body and minute concentrations can have dramatic effects on physiological function. It is during the last 20 years that hormones have been seen to play a major, and often controversial, role in athletics. Along with new understanding of the way in which hormones function came the much publicised drug abuses. It was soon realised that drugs, like the body-building steroids or growth hormone, could dramatically improve athletic performance while other drugs (often used by the 'dopers') slowed a horse's metabolism or inhibited muscle contractions to cause a marked loss of performance.

The mechanism of hormone action is subtle and complex. For example increases in skeletal muscle bulk and efficiency of muscle contraction depend both directly and indirectly on hormone action. One of the most important hormones to the racehorse trainer is Adrenalin.

Fright, Flight or Fight

Adrenalin is secreted by the Adrenal Medulla, a gland that is found attached to the kidneys, and it is also released from specialised nerve endings (the sympathetic nerve terminals). Adrenalin is responsible for the famous 'fright, flight or fight' response in animals. It is secreted along with a similar acting hormone, noradrenaline, and has a number of different effects, some excitatory and some inhibitory, all of which are related to the fright, flight or fight response.

Adrenalin causes the heart to beat quicker and also causes an increase in the diameter of the blood vessels (the arterioles) that take the blood to the contracting muscles. Both effects will increase the ability of the blood to carry oxygen to the muscles and help slow the onset of muscle fatigue. Improved oxygenation of the muscles is also brought about by the action of adrenalin on respiration - in most mammals adrenalin causes an increase in the rate and depth of respiration as well as expansion of the airway passages into the lungs.

Biochemically adrenalin has a powerful effect on the speeding up of the breakdown of muscle and liver glycogen to form ATP for muscle contraction. Adrenalin also accelerates the release of fatty acids from fat stores which is a further source of fuel for muscle contraction.

Adrenalin can cause a significant increase in sweating which helps cool the racehorse. The greater the stress the greater the release of adrenalin and noradrenaline but the quantitative effect of these hormones as a result of training on contracting muscle is extremely hard to assess. Too much stress and the jockey will not be able to control the horse to the best of its ability: too little and the horse 'falls asleep'.

Other Hormones

There are other important classes of 'steroid hormones' which are complex molecules and include hormones like 'progesterone', 'oestrogen', 'cortisone' and 'testosterone'. Testosterone belongs to a class of hormones known as the 'androgens' which influence the 'maleness' of stallions. Testosterone is secreted by the testes and is, in part, responsible for the 'aggressiveness' and 'maleness' of stallions: levels of testosterone increase when a stallion is teased with a mare. Androgens also promote the growth of bone and muscle and they are the anabolic steroids which are sometimes used and abused by athletes for body-building. Jockey Club rules ban the use of anabolic steroids for racehorses.

Progesterone and Oestrogen are hormones that play important roles in the reproductive cycles of mares.

Another important hormone is the 'adrenocorticotrophic' hormone (ACTH) which is secreted by the pituitary gland and causes the adrenal cortex to produce 'corticosteroid hormones' like 'cortisone'. Cortisone has a direct effect on reducing swelling and pain and was at one time widely used in reducing inflammation and swelling of racehorses' joints. However cortisone can damage the articulating surfaces of joints and nowadays to relieve pain and joint swelling trainers use more modern, non-steroid, drugs such as 'bute' - phenylbutazone - which can be given orally.

There are also small molecules known as 'peptide hormones' which are secreted at a number of different sites and, for example, have important regulatory effects on the digestive and the circulatory systems. The recently discovered short peptide molecules 'endorphins' and 'encephalins', which have a similar structure and pain relieving action to drugs like morphine, are produced by the racehorse's brain and spinal cord at times of extreme stress. It has been suggested that 'twitching' a racehorse calms it down because these peptides are released in response to the pain stress of the twitch.

Hormones are carried by the blood which along with the heart make up the circulatory system. The circulatory system plays a major role in the fitness and athletic ability of a racehorse.

Circulatory System

Blood is the horse's internal transport system which carries food from its gut to the liver and hormones to their target sites. It also plays a major role in fighting infection. Amongst the blood's many other roles is carriage of gases and waste materials to, and from, contracting and resting muscles.

There are two types of cells in the blood, red and white cells. The white cells are further subdivided into five groups and each group has a different role to play in combating infection.

Red Cells

The red blood cells are small transparent envelopes which surround a red, oxygen carrying molecule which is known as 'haemoglobin'. They live about 30 days and there are about a thousand red cells for every white cell. The red blood cells carry oxygen to the muscles from the lungs. In the lungs haemoglobin combines with the oxygen in the air to form oxyhaemoglobin and at the muscles the oxygen is taken from the haemoglobin in the red cells for the production of energy by the Aerobic Pathway (see Chapter 1).

Oxygen Requirements in Exercise

It is estimated that even in mild exercise the oxygen requirements of a racehorse can be increased by as much as 500%. Increasing the number (concentration) of circulating red blood cells greatly improves the oxygen carrying power of the blood and there is a special mechanism in exercising horses that brings about a rapid increase in red cell concentration. The spleen, an organ that lies alongside the horse's stomach, contracts and discharges large quantities of red cells into the blood stream.

The Spleen

The spleen is an important organ in the racehorse as it not only produces but also stores red cells. The spleen starts releasing red blood cells as soon as exercise levels increase and skeletal muscle oxygen supplies become critical. In cases of severe oxygen lack, as in maximal exercise, contractions of the spleen reservoir can increase the circulating number of red cells to some 50% above resting levels.

This increase of circulating red blood cells from the spleen and the resultant increase in the ability of the blood to carry oxygen to the muscle cells is another important reason why racehorses should be 'warmed-up' before a race.

Iron and Oxygen Transport

Lack of iron in the racehorse's diet causes a reduction of haemoglobin production. Since oxygen is carried to the muscle cells by haemoglobin in the red cells, there is a subsequent loss in the oxygen carrying ability of the blood. In severe cases of lack of iron the horse becomes 'anaemic'.

But, providing the horse is given sufficient iron, it has been shown (at least for sprinters in training) that following an intensive training programme there is an increase in both the amount of haemoglobin in the blood and the number of circulating red blood cells. Both factors increase the oxygen carrying ability of the blood and favour the Aerobic Pathway, the most efficient means of energy (ATP) production (see Chapter 1).

We have already seen how long term training can improve the density of small blood vessels, the capillaries, that invade the racehorse's muscles. This increase in capillarisation results in an increase in the total blood volume of the horse. This means an improvement in the oxygen carrying capacity of the blood as well as a larger surface area for the oxygen transfer from blood to muscle to occur.

The Racehorse's Heart

The blood containing the red blood cells is pumped around the body by the heart. Arteries carry blood away from the heart and veins carry blood to the heart. The venous blood carries waste products such as lactic acid and carbon dioxide which are formed when energy is being used or created. The heart is composed of muscle fibres that are structurally and functionally somewhere between skeletal and smooth muscle and, like skeletal muscles, the muscles of the heart receive oxygen and generate ATP by the Aerobic and Anaerobic Pathways.

The Heart as a Pump

The heart can be thought of as being made up of two pumps, the left and right sides of the heart, which push blood around the body. The

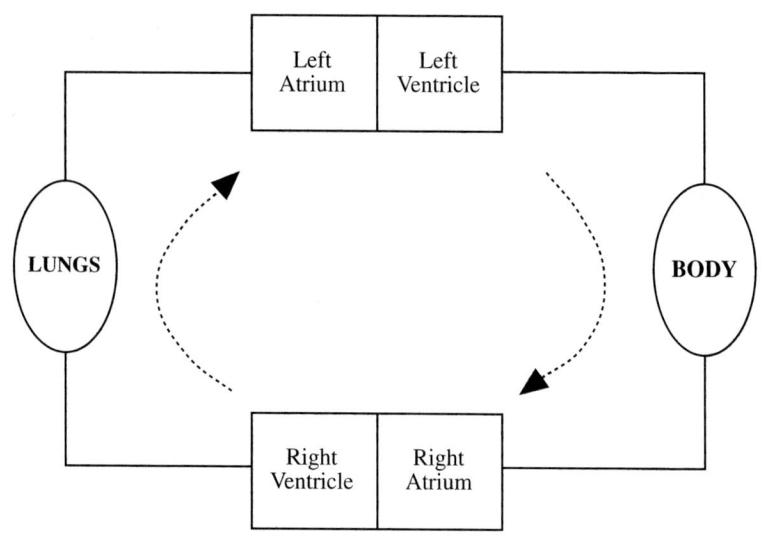

```
                  ┌─────────┬─────────┐
                  │  Left   │  Left   │
                  │ Atrium  │Ventricle│
                  └─────────┴─────────┘
       ╭─────────╮                       ╭─────────╮
       │  LUNGS  │                       │  BODY   │
       ╰─────────╯                       ╰─────────╯
                  ┌─────────┬─────────┐
                  │  Right  │  Right  │
                  │Ventricle│ Atrium  │
                  └─────────┴─────────┘
```

Figure 3.1: The Heart and Circulation.

thoroughbred heart weighs around 9 lbs (4 kg) in pre-trained horses and training can increase the amount of muscular tissue by as much as 50%. The increased muscular size means a greater ability to pump blood and hence deliver oxygen to the racehorse's muscle. It has recently been proposed that racehorse performance is related to heart size. But overtraining can cause the heart muscles to overstretch and eventually weaken.

Heart Anatomy

The right atrium of the heart receives the venous blood which is rich in carbon dioxide from its return from the tissues of the body. The blood is then pumped by the right ventricle to the lungs via the pulmonary artery. In the lungs carbon dioxide is removed and the blood is re-oxygenated. The oxygenated blood returns to the heart via the pulmonary vein to be pumped, by the left ventricle, into the main artery, the aorta. From the aorta blood travels via the other main arteries, arterioles (small arteries) and capillaries to all the tissues of the body.

The ventricles, the lower muscular chambers of the heart, drive out the blood via arteries to the lungs and body tissues while the atria, the two upper chambers of the heart, receive the blood in the veins from

The Art & Science of Racehorse Training CHAPTER THREE

the lungs and tissues. The atria and ventricles are connected to each other by valves which can be heard opening and shutting as the heart beats to drive out the blood some 35 times a minute in the resting horse.

The Heart Beat in Exercise

The heart beat of a horse can be heard on either side of the horse by placing the ear against the rib cage just behind the elbow. After moderate exercise such as walking reasonably quickly round the yard the heart rate can be raised to twice its resting rate. Then the beat can be felt with the palm of the hand when it is placed behind the elbow of either fore limb.

The amount of blood coming out of the heart is known as the 'cardiac output' (CO) and is measured in litres per minute. It depends upon the *amount* of blood coming out of the ventricle per beat (known as the stroke volume (SV) and measured in mls) and the *heart rate* (HR), the number of times the heart beats per minute. Thus CO=SVxHR.

As heart rates in horses can be increased by a factor of eight, compared to less than half this increase in humans, cardiac output is probably less of a limiting factor in supplying oxygen to the working muscles than in trained human athletes.

In racehorses oxygen lack is probably more associated with the malfunctioning of the respiratory system as we shall see later. Trained racehorses show increases in the stroke volume and the cardiac output but their maximum heart rate in severe exercise is unchanged although the heart rate in trained racehorses is probably decreased in moderate exercise.

Heart Rate Meters

There has recently been some interest in the use of newly developed 'non intrusive' heart meters - electronic meters which enable the racehorse's heart rate to be measured whilst undergoing severe exercise. These meters have shown that training does reduce the heart rate for a given speed/work load of a racehorse.

From some experimental evidence using meters it is claimed that at around 150 beats a minute the horse is exercising 'anaerobically' and that this is the trigger for a lactic acid 'threshold' when large amounts of lactic acid are produced. It is believed by some scientists that high lactic acid concentration eventually causes loss of performance by inhibiting skeletal muscle contraction (see Muscle Fatigue, page 8).

The Respiratory System

The respiratory system is responsible for gaseous exchange.

Gaseous Exchange

Blood pumped to the lungs from the right side of the heart is high in carbon dioxide and low in oxygen. 'Gaseous exchange', that is oxygen in to the blood stream, carbon dioxide out, takes place through the walls of the tiny blood vessels, the capillaries, that supply the numerous small balloon like structures that make up the walls of the lungs and which are known as the 'alveoli'.

Training results in an increase in the number of small blood vessels, the capillaries, that lie close to the alveoli. This increase in 'alveoli capillary density' will improve the efficiency of the gaseous exchange process.

The Racehorse's Respiratory Rate

The breathing mechanism has a key role in supplying the alveoli with oxygen and removing carbon dioxide from the lungs, thereby markedly affecting the performance of a racehorse. When breathing in, the diaphragm muscle of the horse contracts along with the muscles in the rib cage. The chest cavity expands drawing air into the lungs. When the muscles relax air is expelled. Inspiration is immediately followed by expiration and then there is a pause. Expiration lasts slightly longer than inspiration and listening to the rhythm of respiration can often give some idea as to the state of health and fitness of the horse.

The respiratory rate (breaths per minute) is about 12 per minute in a resting horse and the rate is easily measured by timing the rise and fall of the horse's flank. The rate is increased by work, high temperatures and stress.

The racehorse breathes in about 10 litres of air with each breath and when the horse is cantering and galloping there is a one to one relationship between respiration rate and the cycle of limb movements.

Expiration is probably mechanically triggered by the front legs striking the ground and expiration continues during the period the front legs are taking the horse's weight. The racehorse lowers its head during expiration.

A cantering horse respires at about 110 breaths per minute and this can increase to around 150 per minute, in a fast gallop if say the horse is covering five furlongs a minute. A galloping horse is completely airborne for a short period and this is approximately the transitory point between the expiration and inspiration phases of respiration. Inspiration starts as the front legs are stretched out forward and the racehorse's head rises, and it continues while the hind legs are in contact with the ground. If expiration is mechanically triggered by the front legs striking the ground the number of strides a horse takes in a minute (strike rate) determines its respiration rate. A tiring horse strikes and breathes at a slower rate.

The Respiratory Passages

The mechanics of the racehorse's respiratory system have recently been scientifically analysed and it is thought by some equine scientists that its anatomy plays a vital role in racehorse performance.

Racehorses breathe through their nostrils (not their mouths) and in a fit, healthy, galloping horse inspiration is soundless while expiration is associated with the well known blowing or trumpeting sound.

Roaring

In respiratory diseases, especially 'roaring', horses make noises when inspiring deeply.

It has recently been suggested that some 95% of all thoroughbreds have some inherited disease of their voicebox and that bleeding from the lungs, or exercise-induced pulmonary haemorrhage (EIPH), which is a very common complaint in severely exercising racehorses, is due to a partial paralysis of the voicebox or some other upper airway obstruction (Cook).

If the horse is a 'roarer' or a 'whistler' through some disease of the voicebox there is not much that can be done. Racehorses can be 'tubed' by pushing a tube, which has to be cleaned each day, down into their tracheae. At one time the so-called 'Hobday' operation was popular but nowadays many trainers question the value of any surgery on the larynx.

In healthy well trained racehorses, even at moderate levels of exercise, there appears to be some impairment in the gaseous exchange mechanism at the alveoli which reduces the amount of oxygen available to the contracting muscles. This impairment might be due to mechanical obstructions of the airways into the lungs at the level of the voicebox.

Choking Up

The nostrils are a continuous part of the 'nasal passages' that run up inside the head of the horse. The nasal passages lead into the larynx or voicebox. The windpipe (trachea), which is about 80 cm long, comes out of the voicebox and feeds into the lungs.

The voicebox is a biological valve which, when open, allows air into the lungs and, when closed, when the horse is swallowing, prevents food from entering the lungs. The larynx is fully open when the racehorse is galloping, letting air pass from the nostrils into the lungs. The larynx is half open when the horse is breathing quietly. The soft palate, a muscular membrane at the back of the nasal chambers, drops down to shut off the air passages from the mouth in the running horse.

'Choking up', sometimes seen in racehorses during a race, is not due to the horse swallowing its tongue but due to the soft palate vibrating and not allowing a proper air flow into the larynx with the result that the horse suddenly becomes short of air and falters.

Airways and Performance

The racehorse's nostril and nasal passages are well adapted for speed. When the horse is galloping its nostrils spread out and act as funnels forcing air into the nasal passages. With speed the airways become more streamlined by the shrinking-back of the lining of the passages. The galloping racehorse extends its neck which further improves airflow. Narrowing of any of the airways or passages into the lungs due to disease or any other factor will seriously affect the performance of a racehorse by eventually limiting the availability of oxygen to the contracting skeletal muscles.

Performance and Airway Anatomy

The anatomical structure of the respiratory system has a direct effect on the flow of air in and out of the lungs. The physical size of a horse's jaw has traditionally been very important when assessing the potential performance of a racehorse - Arabs when buying a horse would put their clenched fists into the horse's throat to test the width behind the jaws. A wide jaw means wide upper airway passages which means that air can more readily enter the lungs of a racehorse than when the jaw is narrow and the upper airway constricted.

It has recently been proposed that a small horse (thus possessing short airway passages), with a wide jaw (thus a good wide upper airway passage) and a wide, large voicebox (the voicebox is a narrow, therefore limiting, part of the upper airway passage) will have three of the most important attributes for speed in a racehorse.

It has also been argued along similar anatomical lines that stayers are stayers because they have less obstructed airways than sprinters. Thus a stayer's skeletal muscles are less oxygen starved than those of a sprinter (Cook).

This simple relationship between airflow and anatomy neatly illustrates how one biological system, the respiratory system, has a direct effect on the muscular system and race track performance of a racehorse.

CHAPTER THREE — *The Art & Science of Racehorse Training*

The winner: a successful interaction of biological systems.

CHAPTER FOUR

Racehorse Biomechanics

A knowledge of the mechanics of racehorse movement, or more properly biomechanics, is vital to the modern day trainer. The more efficiently the energy of skeletal muscle contraction is transferred to the horse's chassis the faster the racehorse. Thus the chassis - the racehorse's skeletal system - has to be in peak condition if the racehorse is to be a winner.

The Bones of the Skeleton

Skeletons are made up of bones. All bone is a living tissue and, like muscles, supplied with arteries, veins and nerves. Growth is through the deposition of calcium phosphate and the growth rate and composition of each bone varies and depends upon the age of the horse and the amount of stress the bone receives. A long bone of the limb for example will grow lengthwise at either end as well as radially and clearly a long narrow limb bone is less strong than a short fat one.

The bone count of a horse changes with time, some bones fusing to form one bone, as does the quality or 'hardness' of the bone. Thus in the growing racehorse it is essential that bone fusion and the proper laying down of hard or 'compact bone' be given time. Limited stress such as walking on hard roads can promote the formation of compact bone in two year olds but these young horses must never be over stressed as their skeletons are still developing and relatively fragile.

The 'Bone' of a Racehorse

Racehorse people often talk about the 'bone' of a horse. This is not really the bone but a measurement of the width (diameter) of the leg taken at a point just below the knee (the metacarpal region, see below). It is used by some as an assessment of the skeletal development of the racehorse, the assumption being that the greater the measurement the 'stronger' the racehorse. While this is true up to a point, light boned racehorses are more likely to 'break down' than heavy boned ones, and the measurement gives no indication of the hardness (density) of the bone which is probably the more important factor.

Developing Bones

In the early stages the bones have the ability to grow faster than the tendons. This is apparent in foals which are fed a rich milk diet, have unlimited other feed and are kept mainly in the stables. The fore feet heels are literally pulled up off the ground by the powerful flexor tendons that are unable to keep up with the growth of the cannon bones - the foal is then said to have 'upright pasterns'. The cure is simple: cut back on the feed; turn out the mare and foal; more exercise; and a less rich, lower calcium diet. This combination will slow growth of bone and soon bring down the fetlock joint. The same upright fetlock effect can occur in yearlings feeding on rich summer pastures and freely available supplementary feed.

Long Bones

The long bones of the limbs can be thought of as the levers that drive the horse's body over the ground. The levers are moved by complex sets of skeletal muscles working in opposition. All muscles work only by contracting. In the simplest case of a joint bending in one direction (as in the elbow or stifle joint) one set of muscles will bend or flex the joint, the flexor muscles, while the other set, the extensor muscles, will straighten or extend it. The more complex the movement the more complex the groups of muscles bringing about the movement and the more complicated is the control mechanism required to bring it about. Most muscles act on two or more bones across a joint, moving one part of the joint on the other so that the joint is thus the centre of rotation.

The Moving Skeleton

Muscles also play an important role in holding joints and, together, ligaments (which are found around the joints) and muscles are often so effective that when stress is applied the bone will break before the joint will give. Together, muscles and tendons, ligaments and bones form a system of levers whose job it is to resist changes due to the weight of the moving racehorse as well as being involved in creating and defining movement around joints.

Joints and Synovial Capsules

The relative movements of limbs take place at joints which can be defined as the meeting place of two or more bones. Not all joints move - for example the joints that connect up the skull bones of a racehorse are immovable and are formed when a spongy tissue, cartilage, becomes invaded with bone. But usually a joint moves and to help movement it is surrounded by a fluid filled capsule, the joint or *synovial capsule*. The oily fluid that fills the capsule is *synovial fluid*.

Tendons and Ligaments

As the skeletal muscles contract the skeleton has to move and joints must operate smoothly and efficiently. Tendons and ligaments play vitally important roles in transmitting the muscle contraction to the bones, encapsulating and moving the joints and tying the bones of the skeleton together.

In the moving horse contracting muscle is attached by one end to a part of the skeleton which does not move while the other end of the muscle is attached to the part which does. The attachment is by tendons, and the part of the muscle which is attached to the non moving part of the skeleton is known as the origin while the other part is known as the insertion. Every fibre in a muscle is attached to a tendon and damage to the tendons (white rope-like inflexible fibres) is one of the most frequent forms of lameness in a racehorse.

More will be said of tendons and ligaments in later chapters as these are, along with primary damage to muscles, constant problems for the racehorse trainer and need to be examined for stress every day. It is important that a racehorse trainer has a good understanding of the structure and function of thoroughbred tendons and ligaments so that any abnormality, usually occurring as a result of training or racing, can be recognised immediately and action taken to avoid permanent lameness.

Tendon Structure and Function

Tendons are covered by a layer (paratenon) in which the blood vessels and nerves that supply the tendon run. The bulk of the tendon is made up of long protein fibres (collagen) which are produced by special cells in the tendon. The fibres are wavy and this helps produce some elasticity in the tendon. As the centre of a tendon is poorly supplied with blood, damaged tendons take a long time to repair and during the repair process they may be replaced with a different type of collagen which is less strong and elastic than the original. The tendons are attached to the bones via a fibrous sheath that surrounds the bones - the periosteum - which is responsible for bone growth.

Tendons may be flattened or in wide sheets and can vary enormously in length. Long tendons allow muscles to act at a distance away from their point of attachment: the tendons of the forearms, for example, run down across the knee to the foot. These tendons as they run close to the surface of the knee are susceptible to injury, especially in young horses where the canals are not fully closed in. For protection tendons run in special canals that are covered with a fibrous material and to reduce friction they are surrounded by special sheaths, filled with synovial fluid which acts as a lubricating liquid.

The Leg Tendons

The upper part of a racehorse's leg has a much higher concentration of skeletal muscle when compared to the lower half. This is in contrast to, for example, the calf muscles of a human. In the racehorse the lower part of the leg is almost devoid of muscle but this has the advantage that the fastest moving part of the leg, (ie the lower part), is lighter and therefore adapted for speed. However keeping the muscles high means that to operate and move the lower leg the tendons have to be long. These long, exposed tendons are thus more vulnerable and susceptible

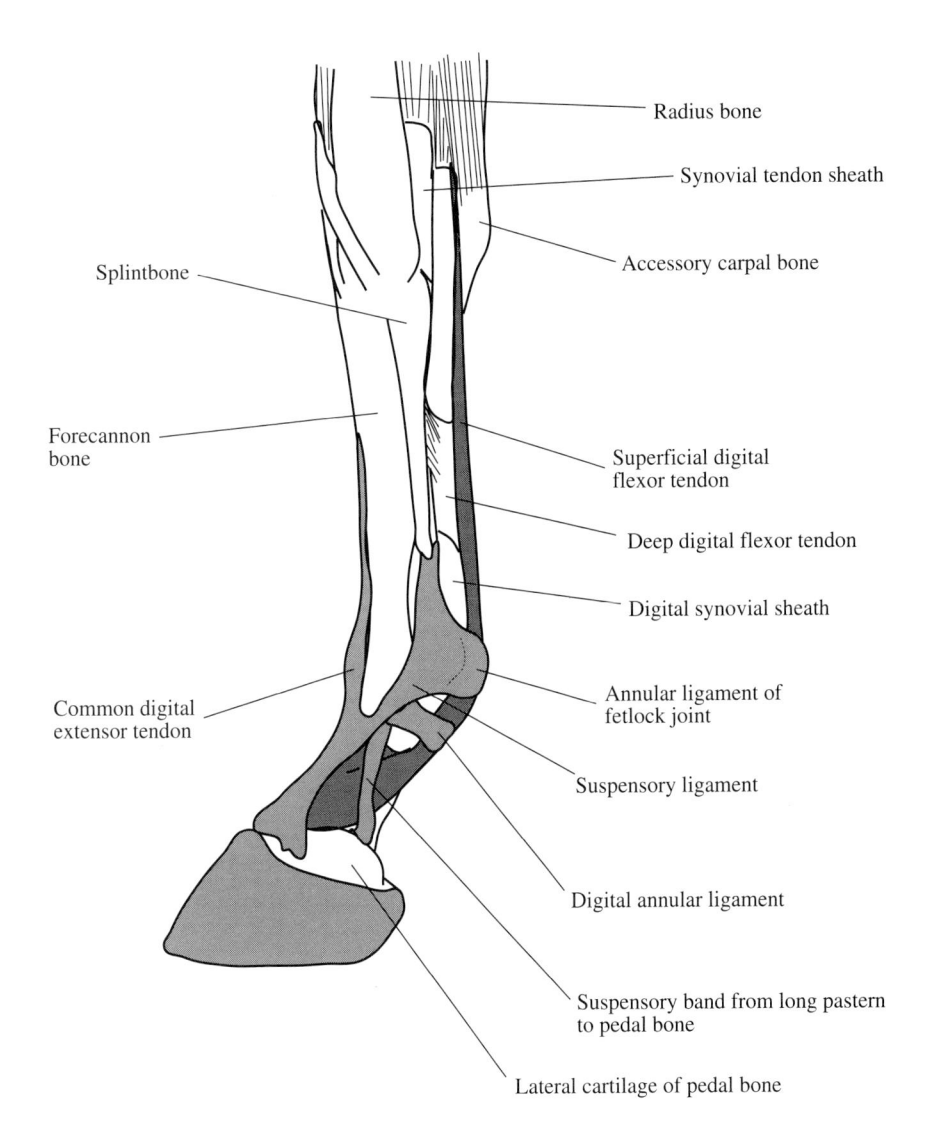

Figure 4.1: Tendons of Inner Forelimb (after P. C. Goody).

to physical damage and strain, when compared to the more deep set tendons of the upper leg.

There are two flexor tendons and one extensor tendon in each leg of a horse. The common digital extensor runs down the front of the foreleg to the pedal bone and, unlike the flexor tendons, is not particularly prone to strains. The superficial digital flexor tendon lies immediately below the skin between the knee or hock and the fetlock. It starts above the knee or hock and is attached to the large superficial flexor muscle before running down the leg behind the knee joint to the fetlock and then becomes flattened. It forms a ring through which the deep flexor tendon runs. Below the fetlock it divides in two and these branches are attached to the long and short pastern bones. The deep (digital) flexor tendon also attaches to a large muscle and runs down the back of the knee or hock in the same canal as the superficial tendon. After passing through the ring of the superficial tendon it passes down the back of the pastern bones, through the two branches of the superficial tendon, outside the navicular bone to finally attach on to the pedal bone (see Figure 4.1).

Some tendons run in special fluid-filled sheaths or sacs. They are generally known as *bursae* and are lubricated by synovial fluid to reduce friction as the limbs move. Some bony points close to the surface are also covered with bursae so that the skin can readily slide over the protuberances. A knock or a blow to the bursae causes them to produce excessive amounts of synovial fluid - a condition known as bursitis. Windgalls of the fetlock joints, bog spavins on the front and thoroughpins on the side of hocks are all examples of an overproduction of synovial fluid.

The bone surfaces of all joints inside a synovial capsule are covered with a layer of cartilage known as the articular cartilage. This cartilage is much more flexible than bone and acts as a buffer for the two faces of the bone, preventing them from chipping. The ball and socket joint of the hip and shoulder joints are examples of capsular joints.

Ligaments

The walls of the capsular joints are made of non muscular tissue known as ligaments - usually yellow coloured fibres that are thicker and more elastic than the tendons. The ligaments help restrict movements of joints in unwanted directions. Some joints, such as the ball and socket joints at the hip and shoulder, allow movements in any direction; other joints, which usually involve bones sliding over each other, for example the elbow and stifle joints, are restricted to movement in only one plane.

Ligaments also have the important role of joining bones together at joints. As a rule ligaments act as preventers to keep joints moving within their normal limits - they are thickest over a joint where there is little movement. The lower limbs of a horse are especially susceptible to sideways flexing and the ligaments help keep the legs in a vertical column. The knee and hock are surrounded by ligaments that restrict the joints to action in one plane. Stretching a ligament beyond its normal limits will cause its fibres to tear and the horse will have a painful sprain. Some ligaments act away from joints, playing important roles like supporting the backbone of the horse, while others form great cords that run down the side of the neck and support the head.

Generally speaking compression and shearing stresses to the skeleton are counteracted by cartilage and bone, and tension stresses by muscles and ligaments.

The Horse's Gait

There are over 200 skeletal bones and some 700 skeletal muscles in the body of a racehorse so it is an extremely complex system of levers and girders. The nomenclature and movement of the limbs is probably best understood by examining the evolution of the horse.

The Evolution of the Horse's Limbs

Horses have evolved over millions of years. They survived by herding and by their ability to flee at great speed when threatened. They are creatures of the plains with long legs, a long neck so that the head can reach the ground, and high centres of gravity. Their bony skeletons have adapted accordingly.

When the primitive fishy vertebrates first crawled out of the sea to the land, the bony skeletons of these precursors of all land animals had to adapt to a life with a downward pull of gravity for they had now lost the upward thrust of the buoyancy of the surrounding water on their bodies. Their centre of gravity, the point at which their body weight appears to act, had now to be taken into account. But first, if they were to stop slithering around on their stomachs, they had to develop limbs to lift themselves off the ground. The result was that the pectoral (chest) and pelvic (hip) fins of these fish-like vertebrates evolved into two pairs of limbs.

With evolution the wriggling limbs moved forward some ninety degrees and then backward to lie parallel with the body so that the feet

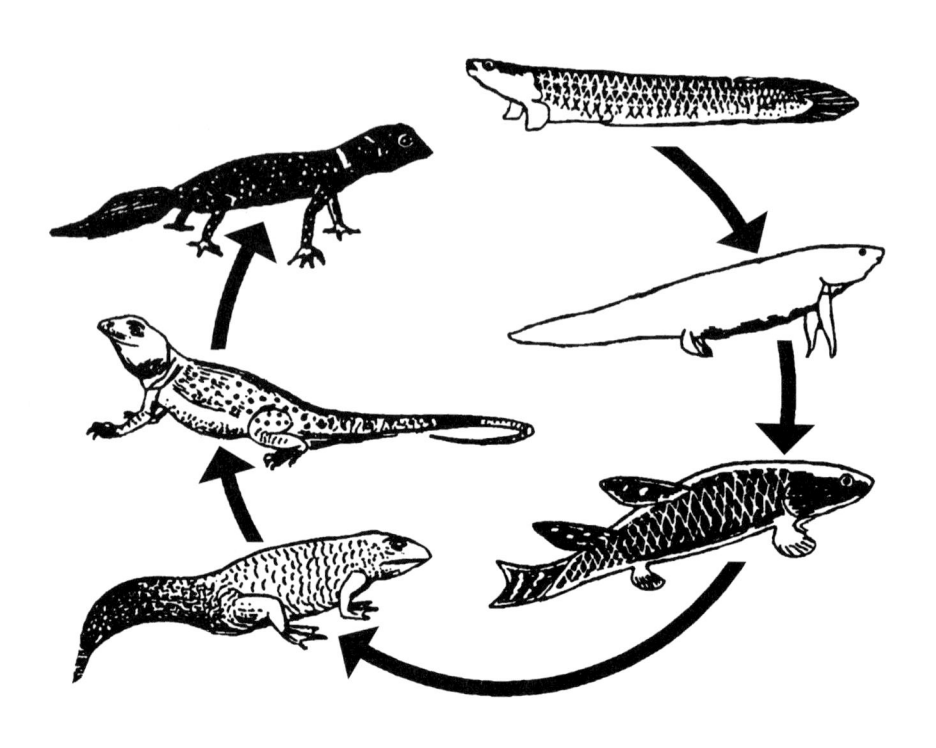

Figure 4.2: Evolution of the Vertebrate Limb (after Grey).

and hands pointed in the same direction as the head. The limbs were jointed and the body pushed off the ground (see Figure 4.2).

Five Digits

The two pairs of limbs of all land vertebrates are based upon a generalised five digit hand and foot (see Figure 4.3). The plan gives much insight into the structure and function of the racehorse by allowing comparisons to be made with the skeletons of other vertebrate mammals. In the generalised skeletal plan each limb is made up of regions that move on each other: the upper arm (thigh) on the forearm (shank) on the wrist (ankle) on the hand (foot).

As the horse evolved from a five digit, marsh-dwelling animal to a fast running creature of the plains, it departed from the generalised five digit (phalange or phalanx) plan to such an extent that it now has only one digit, the third, remaining. Animals run faster when running on their fingers and/or toes. The horse has evolved so that its 'hands' and 'feet' have been raised far off the ground and it walks and runs on the tips of the third finger or toe, that is the third digit, (equivalent to the second finger in man). There is an increase in leverage and power as a result of lengthening the third digit but there is a serious loss of the cushioning effect of the other digits as the third digit strikes the ground. Thus horses, and racehorses in particular, are especially prone to injuries that are brought about by concussive loading - cracked bones, torn ligaments and tendons and strained muscles.

The first digit is lost, the third is longer and stronger and terminates in the hoof and the second and fourth digits have disappeared becoming the almost functionless splint bones that lie along the cannon bones. Thus the splint bones are equivalent to metacarpals (metatarsals) two and four respectively. The medial and lateral splint bones are almost vestigial in that they carry very little weight and damage to these bones is less serious than to almost any other bone in the racehorse's skeleton. The pedal bone is the third digit or phalanx, the short pastern or coronary bone is the second phalanx, the long pastern is the first phalanx. The forecannon and hindcannon are the third metacarpal and metatarsal respectively (see Figure 4.3).

CHAPTER FOUR   *The Art & Science of Racehorse Training*

Fore Limbs (near side) view.

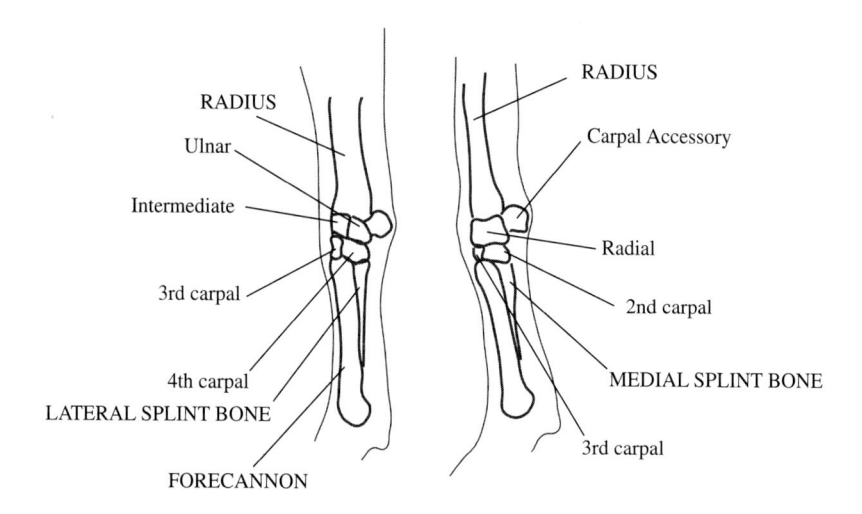

RADIUS
RADIUS
Ulnar
Carpal Accessory
Intermediate
Radial
3rd carpal
2nd carpal
4th carpal
MEDIAL SPLINT BONE
LATERAL SPLINT BONE
3rd carpal
FORECANNON

Hind Limbs (near side) view.

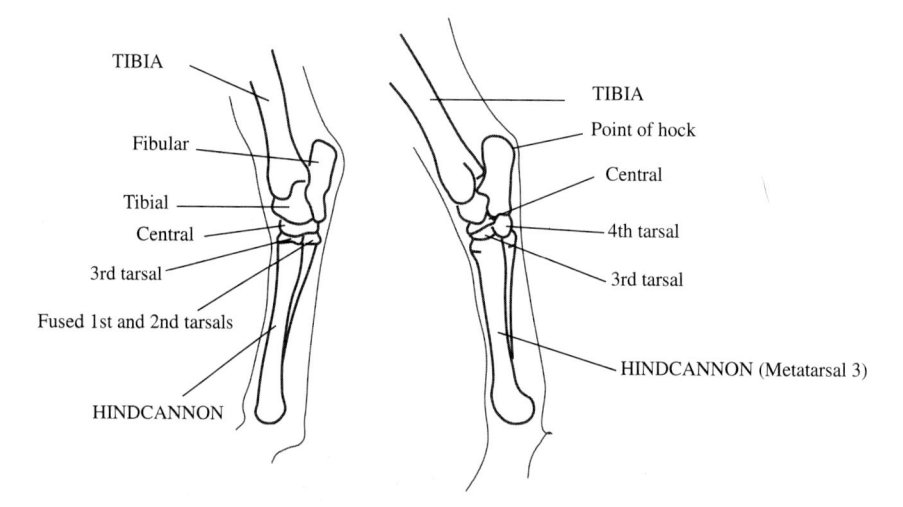

TIBIA
TIBIA
Fibular
Point of hock
Tibial
Central
Central
4th tarsal
3rd tarsal
3rd tarsal
Fused 1st and 2nd tarsals
HINDCANNON (Metatarsal 3)
HINDCANNON

Figure 4.3: Evolved Horse's Limbs.

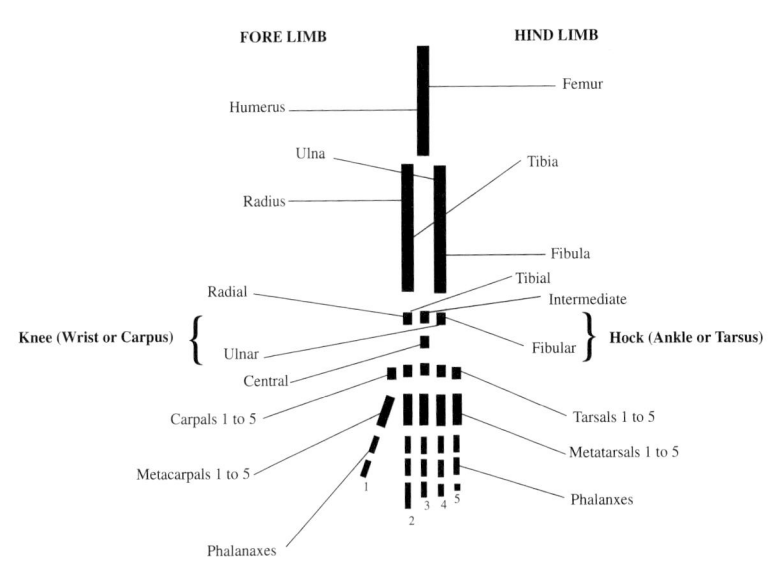

The Art & Science of Racehorse Training CHAPTER FOUR

```
            FORE LIMB              HIND LIMB
                                      ——— Femur
                  Humerus ———
                         Ulna ———
                                      ——— Tibia
               Radius ———
                                      ——— Fibula
                                    Tibial
                  Radial ———      ——— Intermediate
Knee (Wrist or Carpus) {  Ulnar ———     Fibular  } Hock (Ankle or Tarsus)
                  Central ———
                  Carpals 1 to 5 ———    ——— Tarsals 1 to 5
                                        ——— Metatarsals 1 to 5
           Metacarpals 1 to 5 ———
                                        ——— Phalanxes
                  Phalanxes ———
```

Figure 4.3: Generalised Five Digit Plan.

Early Movement

The first terrestrial limbs probably stuck out at right angles to the body and, to move, the early two-limbed vertebrates wriggled over the soil in such a way that, when the fore limb of one side moved forward, the hind limb of the opposite side also moved forward. Even with the limbs moving forward and lifting the body off the ground (and despite evolution creating many different types and forms of animals) this original wriggling means of locomotion has evolved into a well defined walking pattern for all animals with two pairs of limbs. When the fore foot of the left side moves forward there is a corresponding forward movement of the rear foot on the right side, the diagonal leg, and vice versa. The crocodile is a good example of this walking pattern, the horse a bad example because its pattern of locomotion is complicated and depends on its speed.

Although the racehorse exhibits many variations of gait, there are four well known basic gaits (see also Smythe and Goody):

The Moving Horse

The Trot
The trot is a classical two limbed vertebrate movement, a 'two time gait' with diagonal pairs of legs hitting the ground together.

The Walk
The walk is a 'four time gait' (one–two: three–four) where all four feet hit the ground separately. A foot is lifted as soon as another in the walking sequence touches the ground. The horse has two or three feet on the ground and in the normal walk the horse balances itself on two feet on the same side and then on two diagonally opposed feet.

The Canter
In the canter, a 'three time gait', either rear limb can hit the ground first, this is followed by the second hind limb and the diagonal foreleg which hit the ground simultaneously. Finally the other foreleg hits the ground. The final foreleg is the 'leading leg' and points the horse in this direction as it moves forward in the canter.

The Gallop
The gallop is a 'four time gait' and similar to the canter except that all four feet strike the land separately. In a flat out gallop the limbs are bent when they move forward and then straightened as they are moved back for the power stroke. The foot strikes the ground at maximum backward velocity when the limb is vertical. Then maximum forward drive is imparted to the horse's body just after the limb is past the vertical.

Centre of Gravity
Because of its head and long neck, a resting horse's centre of gravity, (ie. the point at which its weight can be said to act) lies nearer the

forelimbs than the hindlimbs - about a third of the distance between fore and hindlimbs. Resting horses are often seen with one hind leg resting off the ground. They are able to do this without falling over as there is still a triangle of support with the two forelegs and the other hind leg. Racehorses can also kick with either hind leg without falling over. If, however, a forefoot is lifted the horse has to shift its centre of gravity backwards to prevent itself from toppling. The head and neck are supported by the front legs and by moving the neck up and back the horse can shift its weight back towards the hind legs so that it becomes more 'in balance'. In the extreme case rearing or standing on its back legs pulls the centre of gravity right back.

The centre of gravity must move back over the hind legs when a racehorse suddenly applies power to its hindlimbs when, for example, it moves out of the starting stalls. The drive of the hindlimbs can be so violent that this rapid movement of the weight makes the fore legs lift well off the ground with the result that the racehorse is left behind at the start of the race!

The Spine as a Girder

The spine or vertebral column of the horse can be seen as a semi rigid girder which carries the weight of the body. The spine is supported at each end by the limbs and shoulder and hip joints and is a horizontally rigid structure although there are up and down movements taking place at the loins. Because of this the horse is unable to execute tight turns by simply flexing its spine, relying on its ability to pivot on its hind legs in a confined space.

When the back or spine is subjected to compression the individual vertebrae are cushioned from each other by the inter-vertebral discs which also help resist the crushing forces. As the back is stretched, the muscles, tendons and ligaments that connect the vertebrae to themselves and to the fore and hindlimbs help resist the increase in tension.

When racing the horse will negotiate long bends at the race track by intuitively taking larger strides with the outer limbs. A horse galloping hard thus pulls towards the leading leg which is always the inside leg when it is travelling around a corner. (A racehorse changing leading legs is a frequent cause of a horse suddenly veering to its other side and thus causing a collision in a race.) The head and neck are also used to help direct the racehorse round the bend.

The Hindlimbs

The hindlimbs are directly attached to the spine via the pelvic girdle. The pelvic girdle, a hollow bone section, can be thought of as a rigid box girder that transmits thrust up from the driving hindlimbs through to the spine. The disadvantage of such a system is that any concussive loads from the hind legs are also transmitted directly to the spinal column.

The hindlimbs are the main propulsive power units in the racehorse because of their large muscle mass and bony attachment to the spinal cord. They can be likened to coiled springs that project thrust from the muscles of the back legs through to the spinal column.

Horses hindlimbs do not travel forwards a long way because of the rigidity of the spinal column and the anatomy of the bony joints of the pelvic girdle. Muscles and ligaments further limit the forward movements of the limbs.

The Forelimbs

Because of the weight of the head and neck, the forelimbs have to support more weight than the hindlimbs in both the resting and moving horse. In a jumping horse the forelegs have to withstand a force far greater than the body weight of the horse when it jumps and lands on one leg. It is not surprising then that lameness is more common in the forelimbs of racehorses than the hindlimbs.

The forelimb of the horse is not tied to the horse's body by a bony joint, unlike the hindlimbs' attachment to the pelvic girdle, but the wide shoulder blade is held in place by muscles and ligaments. This has the advantage in that the forelimb attachment of the horse is more flexible than that of the hindlimb and is better adapted to withstand the greater concussive loads it is subject to.

Concussive Loading

The front legs are particularly susceptible to stress when the racehorse is in motion, especially when running fast over hard ground or landing after completing a jump. The forelimbs of the horse behave more like shock absorbers and to this end, starting with the non-bony attachment of the scapula to the body, the entire forelimb has evolved into a very clever and complex shock absorbing system.

After completing a jump and before landing, both forelimbs are outstretched in front of the horse. Just before touchdown one of the legs is dropped and the total weight of horse plus jockey comes down on the fetlock of this leg - a load that can easily exceed half a ton (500 kg). Not surprisingly the fetlock gives and in some cases the ergot will touch the ground.

The downward movement of the fetlock is counteracted by the suspensory ligaments and the flexor tendons (which are attached to the pedal bone) acting as 'extended springs' in the shock absorbing front legs (see Figure 4.5). The suspensory ligament, which is not a true ligament but a modified non-contracting muscle, runs from close to the knee, down behind the cannon bone, before branching into two and attaching to the two sesamoid bones behind the fetlock. (The suspensory ligaments' other important role is to maintain the horse's posture at rest.) Small ligaments go from the sesamoid bones to the back of the long pastern bone. Branches of the suspensory ligament run down from the sesamoid bones to eventually join the digital extensor tendon that runs down the front of the leg (see Figure 4.5).

The flexor muscles which lie at the back of the legs are in slight tension when the horse is at rest, helping to maintain posture. As the load on the leg is increased the flexor muscles help cushion the effect of the load by a controlled lowering of the fetlock. The flexor muscles drive the leg up by contracting when the horse starts to apply the power stroke to lift up the fetlock. There are no muscles below the knee of the horse and the flexor (and extensor) muscles act through long tendons that run down from above the knee or hock. As the flexor muscles contract they pull on the pedal bone and pastern and fetlock joints and the horse's leg straightens. The front part or toe of the hoof acts as the fulcrum for the downward thrust of the load and upward pull of the flexor muscles. The toe of the hoof thus wears out more quickly than the heel of the hoof.

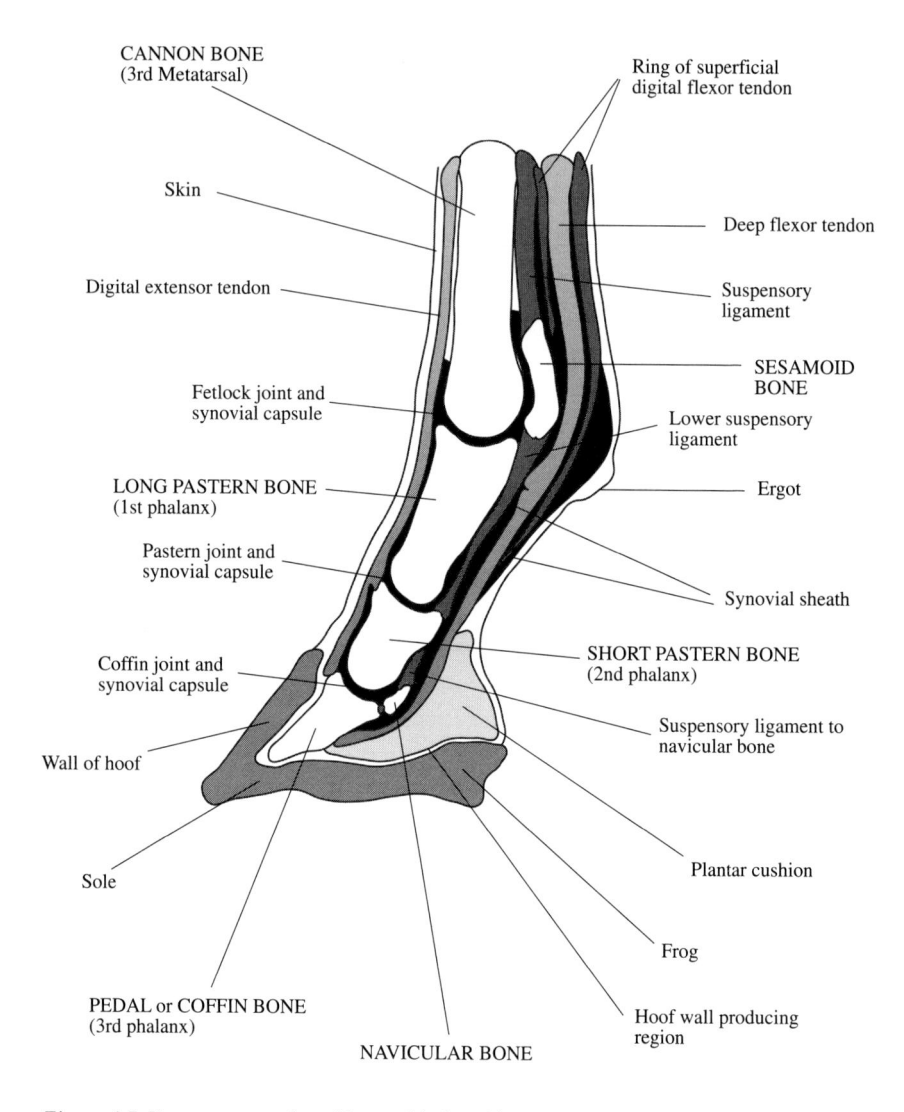

CHAPTER FOUR   *The Art & Science of Racehorse Training*

Figure 4.5: Transverse section of Lower Limb, mid cannon to hoof *(after P. C. Goody)*.

The Plantar Cushion

The load on the feet from the fore and hindlimbs is transferred to a specially modified part of the hoof, known as the plantar or heel cushion, by the long and short pastern bones (see Figure 4.5). The plantar cushion, which is full of fatty fibrous tissue, acts like a solid rubber ball in the hoof of the racehorse as it receives and dissipates the concussive loadings from the limbs. There are special cartilages (the lateral cartilages) which are connected to the plantar cushion and these cartilages are forced apart to further spread the load.

The Racehorse's Foot

Compared to other less fleet breeds the racehorse's feet are usually smaller, lighter and more square. The outside of the foot of the racehorse is insensitive, like the finger nails in man, and made of horn that is derived from the skin that encloses the pedal and part of the second pastern bones. The outside horn is secreted by the coronary band at the rate of about 12 cm a year. The frog, a horny cushion on the underneath of the foot, is made of softer more elastic horn than the side walls of the hoof. The frog and the sole come from a special membrane that lies under the pedal bone. In an unshod horse the 'bars' (which are an upturned part of the horny outside wall) take some of the horse's weight and, if the ground is soft, the frog can also take weight. The sole does not touch the ground and is further off the ground in the hind feet than in the fore. If the sole becomes damaged or overfull of horny material it can cause lameness in the racehorse. A horse's front feet, being flatter, are more susceptible to bruising and some racehorses are more 'flat-footed' than others and thus more susceptible to bruising.

The Resting Horse

Muscles and ligaments play an important role in supporting the skeleton when the horse is at rest. Horses are able to stand still and relax due to specially developed 'check' and suspensory ligaments as well as a number of muscles whose role is to lock the horse's joints in the fore and hindlimbs. This system of muscles and ligaments is known as the stay apparatus.

The Stay Apparatus

The stay apparatus is different in both fore and hindlimbs but below the knee or hock both limbs make use of the suspensory ligament, the long ligament that runs down the leg behind the cannon bone. Its upper end is attached to the back of the knee joint and the top of the cannon bone and its lower end is attached to the digital extensor tendon that runs up the front of the leg (see Figure 4.5).

Check ligaments run from bone to tendon (as opposed to bone to bone) and act as a semi-elastic support to muscle tendons which are relatively non elastic. The superficial and deep flexor tendons are limited by check ligaments. In both fore and hindlimbs above the knee or hock the stay apparatus is maintained by a system of muscles.

Conclusion

In the last four chapters the racehorse's muscles, fuel, blood, breath and bones have been examined in some detail. An understanding of this is essential for the modern day trainer. The racehorse is indeed a complex biological machine. Henry James Rous writing over a hundred years ago summed up the difficult task facing any modern day trainer:

There are very few horses which require the same work, the same food, or the same physic. Thickwinded horses with strong constitutions may be sweated every five days during their preparation, and will take three times as much work as some delicate mares or geldings, of which there are many which never sweat. One horse cannot gallop when the ground is deep; another, with thin feet, cannot move if the ground is hard; and a heavy fall of rain will often upset scientific calculations. Mares seldom run in their best form before the month of August and geldings are considered to be best in spring. Taking, therefore, into consideration the differences of opinion respecting individual condition, the effect of weight on the comparative qualifications of the horses engaged, the possible indisposition of some of them, the unequal merits of the jockeys, and the uncertain state of the ground, it is not to be wondered at that some races resolve themselves into problems difficult of solution; and this constitutes the greatest interest in racing, or what is called 'the glorious uncertainty of the Turf'.

Despite the many advances of science over the last hundred years, the Turf is as 'uncertain' today as it ever was.

CHAPTER FIVE

Stablecraft

Racehorses take a keen interest in their surroundings.

Much of the art and science of racehorse training takes place in and around the stable. The structure of a stable, mucking out, grooming, bedding, shoeing, clipping and many other tasks, which to the outsider may seem menial, are essential parts of the art and science of racehorse training. Stablecraft is as important in developing the full potential of a racehorse as are the trainer's exercise regimes.

Disease and Failure

Sometimes racehorses dramatically fail to live up to their trainer's and owner's expectations. Bill Marshall believes that about half of these inexplicable failures at the race course are due to two problems that arise in the stables. One is the result of a virus that runs undetected through all the stabled horses and the other, probably less important, is due to bacterial diseases that are carried by mice and rats and are picked up by the horses, often in their feed.

Bacterial Infections

Rodent droppings are a particularly potent source of enterobacteria (Salmonella) which can give the racehorse diarrhoea; this is very difficult to eradicate and can be quickly fatal. A secondary bacterial infection often occurs because of an initial viral attack and, unlike many bacteria, viruses are resistant to treatment by antibiotic drugs. To date over 50 types of viruses have been identified in horses and while most are not dangerous some can give rise to unpleasant viral infections which are often very difficult to detect as there are no primary symptoms. Racehorse viral diseases are not normally passed to humans.

Viruses

Viruses are probably the oldest form of living matter and one of the simplest as they consist of DNA (deoxyribonucleic acid) molecules or RNA (ribonucleic acid) molecules surrounded by a protein or fat sheath. DNA carries the genetic information in all cells in the form of genes. DNA is made up of two long molecules that are interconnected to form a double helix which is created when the two molecular strands coil around each other. The connecting chemical molecules that link the two long molecules together in the double helix are known as 'bases' and the bases give rise to the 'genetic code' which is responsible for all the inherited characteristics of any living organism.

RNA is similar in chemical make–up to DNA but is a single stranded molecule. Within a living cell the genetic code inherent in the DNA molecule is passed on to the RNA which is then responsible for the synthesis of protein. Proteins are molecules that carry out many important structural, hormonal and defence roles within all living organisms. The invading virus takes over this RNA/protein manufacturing apparatus of the living cells to produce new viruses which are eventually released from the cell often along with toxins. The new viruses bring about the host cells' destruction - often bursting the cell wall or membrane as they break out of the host cell.

Thus viruses can only replicate themselves in living cells and are even small enough to infect bacteria. A bacterium is around one thousandth of a millimetre (c. 1 micrometer) while a viron measures as little as a hundred thousandth of a millimetre (c. 10 nanometres). Before entering the host body as a parasite, viruses may exist for long periods of time at an inert stage waiting to be carried to their host cells by a variety of means.

Viral Infections

It is the virus' ability to replicate itself inside a host's cells that makes it relatively immune to the host's normal bodily defence mechanisms. Viral infections are thus dangerous and difficult to eradicate with conventional drugs because the drugs cannot attack the virus in its active phase without first entering the host's cells and perhaps interfering with the cells' fundamental biochemistry.

Inoculating Racehorses

Viruses can be attacked by the invaded body's defence mechanisms when the viruses are in the host's blood stream or tissue before they enter the host's cells or after the viruses are released into the blood stream by destroyed or disintegrating host cells. Circulating in the horse's blood stream are white blood cells which engulf and destroy the invading viruses. Other defence mechanisms produced by the host are 'antibodies', small chemical particles that combine with the viruses and any viral toxins to make them harmless.

Inoculation is a successful way of preventing viral infections. It is so effective against equine influenza that today inoculation against influenza is a requirement for any horse that enters a racecourse. The principle of inoculating racehorses against viruses is based upon the horse producing antibodies to an infection. The horse is 'challenged' by an inactive form of the virus (inoculated) and produces antibodies which are then ready to attack the live, active virus when it attacks the horse. A horse that has been challenged more readily produces antibodies to an invading virus than one that has not been challenged.

Stabling and Infection

The stabling of a race horse is one of the key aspects of its training. In order to avoid viral and bacterial infections, as well as for the general well being of a horse, each stable should be clean, dry, well ventilated, free from draughts and full of natural light.

A Healthy Stable

A healthy stable has through ventilation which is best obtained by having a window at one end of the box and the opening, top half of the stable door at the other. The opening window should be of reinforced, frosted glass to prevent young horses attempting to jump through. The window should have hinges on its bottom edge so that it slopes inward when open and the through air flow is directed towards the roof of the stable and not directly over the horse. The window should still be capable of being fully opened so that a good through breeze can be obtained to air the stables or cool them when the weather is hot.

Bill Marshall was once contract trainer to the late William Hill at Whitsbury and believes that these were ideal stables. The stable block was made up of loose boxes built parallel to each other and laid out in a 'U' shape. The stable doors opened on the inside of the U with direct access to the yard, and windows were at the opposite end of the box. He is very much against the type of stabling (American barns) where all the horses are kept under one roof and when stalls are used instead of boxes. This stabling produces a 'fug and a smell of urine and ammonia', conditions that are 'ripe for cross infection', when one horse becomes infected, and most or all of the horses will then pick up the same infection. In American barns ventilation is often inadequate and supplied by fans in the roof of the building which pull air and fumes through the stables, further spreading airborne diseases.

A Proper Box

Each box should be at least 12 feet wide, 12 feet long and around 10 feet high, to give some 1,500 cubic feet of volume per horse. Providing that the doors and windows can be shut to keep out the draughts there is no need to supply heating in temperate climates - extra warmth can easily be supplied with additional horse rugs. In temperate climates, for maximum warmth and light, it is best if the inside of the U-shaped stable block faces south.

Stable Doors

The stable doors should be made of wood, always open outwards into the yard, split horizontally and at least four feet wide. The bottom part of the door should be around four feet six inches high and held in place with two external bolts. The top door should be about a foot shorter than the bottom door and have two bolts, one on the inside and one on the outside. And, most importantly, the top door must have a secure means of holding it in the open position to avoid the wind swinging the top door on to a horse's head. It is an important part of the social life and well-being of a racehorse to be able to look over the stable door and see the other horses and the yard's activities.

An over-hanging stable roof is best so that during rain the top half of the stable doors can remain open, the horses can continue to look out and the grooms are able to walk under the over-hanging roof to continue their work in dry conditions.

Floor

The floor of the stable should be made of concrete as this surface is easily cleaned. A good thick covering of bedding will prevent the horse from slipping and dry, clean bedding is very important for the well-being of the horse.

Bedding

Racehorses, excitable animals, often prefer to urinate or 'stale' when they are quiet and in familiar surroundings, which usually means their stables and one of the important tasks of stable bedding is to soak up this urine.

CHAPTER FIVE   *The Art & Science of Racehorse Training*

Healthy bedding for healthy racehorses.

Bright, dust-free and yellow wheat straw does make the warmest bedding but it is expensive, it does not soak up urine well and it is difficult to obtain in Britain.

Horses are rarely seen lying down in a stable but a thick bedding will encourage them which can help horses with bad legs.

Wood shavings, sawdust and chopped or shredded paper are known as 'litter materials' and make viable alternatives to straw but they are not as warm, they are less easy to muck out and they are unsuitable for selling on as manure. Wood shavings are a good choice, provided they are clean and relatively dust free, as they are the easiest to handle. It is possible to mix a litter material with straw, laying one of them down as an absorbent layer under the straw. This is especially useful if there is a problem with drainage in the stable.

Chronic obstructive pulmonary disease is one of the most frequent causes of 'coughing' in racehorses. It is due to dust or fungus spores in the straw bedding and usually begins to affect horses as two year olds when they can become allergic to spores and dust. Thus dust-free, litter-type bedding is useful if a racehorse is prone to coughing.

Mucking Out

The stables should be mucked out every day before the horses are 'tacked up' for their morning exercise. Whenever a groom enters a stable any fresh dung should be picked up to avoid treading it into the bedding. Poor mucking out techniques and failure to 'pick up' can result in expensive bedding being wasted.

To muck out, the groom should first remove the urine-soaked bedding and fresh dung. Straw bedding should be turned over with a pitchfork and the droppings and short broken straws shaken free to be swept up later. The bedding should be piled in one corner of the stable and then respread replacing old bedding with fresh straw from the barn. When relaying the straw the groom must make sure that the oldest straw which is best for soaking up the urine, lies on the stable floor. The new straw is mixed with some old which helps prevent the horse from eating the fresh straw. If there is a shortage of bedding the straw can be put out in the sun to dry and swept back in at night. Each day after 'afternoon stables' the droppings are picked up, any wet bedding removed and replaced and the bed forked over for the night.

If using a litter material for bedding it can be kept in place by putting a removable six inch plank across the stable entrance, which the horse soon becomes used to stepping over. Mucking out requires the removal of the dung and damp litter. The litter should be turned each day to prevent compacting and any wet litter replaced. It is important that litter bedding is kept dry and clean for it soon becomes damp and malodorous.

Disinfecting

Stables should be disinfected once a week. This requires removing the horse and then all the bedding to a spare box. The concrete floor is swilled down with water and disinfectant. The box is swept out and any remaining water should be soaked up with sprinkled sawdust. The floor must be thoroughly dry before the bedding and the horse are returned.

Feed Store and Tack Room

In the ideal situation the feed store and the tack or saddle-room are respectively at the bottom two corners of a U shaped stable block. At

CHAPTER FIVE — *The Art & Science of Racehorse Training*

Whitsbury, for example, the trainer's house faced the inside of the U and his office was next to the house.

The feed store in any yard must be dry and capable of being locked and the food bins should be rat and mice proof. The saddle or tack room needs to be dry, airy and to have as many cupboards and shelves as possible for all the many 'bits and pieces' that training requires. There should be a locked medicine cabinet and lines of strong hooks and pegs. The room should be kept clean and, in temperate climates,

A tidy tack room where everything has its place.

heated. It should be kept tidy with the saddles stored on saddle posts, the breast-plates, reins, bridles and bits on the hooks and the bandages disinfected, clean, rolled and stored in or on lockers. The horse restrainers - the 'twitch' and the 'Long Tom' - should be ready to hand.

The Exercise Tack

Saddles, bridles and reins should be cleaned and dried after use. That is why a warm, dry, tack room is essential in cold damp climates. The exercise saddles are heavier than the flat racing saddles and weigh about seven pounds. The exercise tack should be light and strong and a mounted exercise saddle with girth, irons and leathers should not weigh more than 10 lbs.

Tropical Stabling

Stabling racehorses in the tropics is very similar to temperate climates. The main emphasis should be on the stables being clean, dry, cool and airy. A yard that has plenty of tree shade is an advantage for the well being of both the horses and the training staff.

Air Conditioned Stables

Air conditioned stables should never be used for stabling racehorses in the tropics. The horse is locked away in a damp, sometimes cold, airtight box and the air conditioning filters, which soon become clogged, make ideal breeding grounds for bacteria. The sudden changes of temperature when going from inside to out are not good for the general health of the horse and, perhaps the worst aspect of all, the locked away horses will suffer from 'confinement' or 'isolation stress'. Racehorses are herd animals and in the wild have complex patterns of communication. They 'enjoy' seeing other horses and take an interest in the activities in the yard. They appreciate the chance to look over their stable doors and a healthy racehorse is an alert and interested animal.

In the tropics, stables should be installed with overhead fans that are situated as high as possible in the ceiling. The higher the fan the better as this tends to keep the dust levels down and the on/off fan switches must be placed well away from the reach of the horse's mouth (as with

Shade is important in a tropical yard.

the electric light switches). The fan should be kept running all the time and the stable windows are always left open and, if necessary, covered with bars or steel mesh. The top of the stable doors are left open wherever possible. The aim is to ensure that fresh air is constantly being circulated through the stable and the horse kept cool.

In the tropics (and in temperate climates) the stables should be lit with an electric bulb of around 100 watts which is encased in a strong glass covered holder inside a grill mesh. Lighting in a stable should not be too bright but obviously bright enough to be able to bandage a leg or inspect a cut. Bright, fluorescent, overhead strip lighting stresses horses.

In the tropics it is almost impossible to obtain straw for bedding, and the trainer has to rely on what is locally available. In Barbados, for example, Bill Marshall uses shredded paper, wood shavings, a local dried, coarse grass or the shredded remains of pulped sugar cane.

Grooming

An important part of keeping racehorses healthy and in top condition is grooming. It keeps a racehorse's skin healthy and clean, the sweat pores unblocked for exercise and the oil glands healthy to produce a smooth and glossy coat. Regular grooming also cleans away all the loose dead skin and massages, stimulates and tones the underlying blood vessels and muscles.

Racehorses should be groomed three times a day. A quick brush over in the morning before exercise, a good wash down and brush after exercise and a thorough groom before evening stables. Horses enjoy being groomed if the grooming is done with care and attention to their well-being.

Bill Marshall likes the grooms (men or women) to start at the head and gently sponge out eyes, nostrils and lips. Then a soft bristled body brush should be forced through the coat of the neck, body and rump of the horse, the groom easing their weight into the stroke and standing away from the horse so that the groom's full weight can be brought to bear on the brush through the arms. Grooming with the body brush should be hard work.

The thin-skinned, bony parts of the body, such as the head and under the belly, should be brushed much more gently than the rest of the body, special care being taken not to bang the horse's under belly. The body-brush should be occasionally cleaned with a rubber 'curry comb' to remove hair, scurf and dirt from the brush.

Next the mane and tail should be brushed out gently with the stiffer, longer-bristled dandy brush and the dock and anus sponged with a different sponge from the one used on the head. The legs are brushed down and the feet picked out with a hoof-pick. The groom, to get the horse to lift up its leg so the underside of the hoof can be cleaned, should first run a hand down the front of the leg from as high as the shoulder or quarter before picking up the pastern with one hand and operating the pick with the other.

The frog should be cleaned, checked for cuts or bruises and the hooves oiled with sump oil. The oil also might prevent the hooves from cracking, although there is not much scientific evidence to support this. Over the years Bill Marshall has used various different greases and oils but finds that old engine sump oil is as good as any proprietary brand! In temperate climates Marshall oiled the racehorses' feet before sending them out to exercise in wet weather. It is important that the hoof is cleaned after exercise and racehorses are not allowed to stand around with their soles full of damp mud.

During grooming the elbows of the horse's legs should also be greased with Vaseline to prevent hard lumps, 'sleeping elbow', from appearing. The groom should immediately inform the trainer if there are any problems with the horse's feet or its shoes.

The Racehorse's Feet

It is essential that a racehorse has healthy feet and horse's feet require constant attention. A racing stable must have a good blacksmith or farrier in constant attendance. A farrier can improve a horse's action as much as months of training and is thus as important to a trainer as a good work rider or jockey.

A racehorse's hoof grows about 1 cm a month and it takes about a year for the horn growing out of the coronary band to reach the bottom of the hoof. In an unshod horse the weight is taken on the bars, walls and frog of the horse, with most of the weight falling on the insensitive horny wall (see page 48). In a correctly shod horse standing on a hard level surface, weight falls on the walls of the hoof, but on soft ground the bars and the frog may just touch the ground. The shoe should spread the horse's weight as much as possible so the 'white line' (the softer horny junction that lies between sole and outside hoof wall) is usually covered by the shoe.

Shoeing

During movement the heel of the foot hits the ground first and the plantar cushion and frog swell as the concussive loads come on the foot (see page 48). The wall at the heel also swells. As the hoof tilts forward the sole flattens and the slightly elastic horny wall and white line take some of the outward movement of the downward thrust of the horse's weight. The hoof tilts forward due to the contracting flexor muscles pulling upwards on the pedal bone and the toe of the hoof is the last part to leave the ground. The shoe is attached to the toe and wall of the hoof with a gap left for the heel of the foot to expand and contract as the load comes on and off the foot.

Horseshoes should be an even width throughout their length even though the width of the horn of the foot tends to be thicker at the toe than the heel of the foot. Looking from the side of the horse, the horn is higher at the toe than at the heel and the correct downward slope of the front of the hoof (to avoid excessive strain on tendons and ligaments) should be approximately continuous with an imaginary line drawn down the front of the pastern. The angle the line down the front of the pastern makes with the ground should be the same as the angle an imaginary line drawn down the front of the hoof makes with the ground. The horn of the feet should be trimmed to keep this angle.

It is very important when training racehorses that the horn of the foot is kept properly trimmed and the foot maintained 'in balance' so that the toe is not too long or the heel too short, otherwise excessive strain will be put on the tendons. Whenever a new shoe is fitted it should be made to fit the foot and not the foot made to fit the shoe. Excessive paring and rasping of the hoof should always be avoided. The fitted shoe must lie flat and follow the outline of the hoof wall.

Exercise Plates

In temperate climates racehorses are shod for exercise as they are often exercised on roads to and from the canter tracks and gallops. Iron shoes are best for exercise. A light iron shoe of about six or seven ounces (c. 150g) should be fitted cold. A good farrier can always work the shoe cold so that it becomes a perfect fit. (The traditional practice of fitting a hot (dull, red) shoe by burning the shoe into the foot when 'hot shoeing' can give rise to many problems for the trainer. An unskilled farrier will burn unlevel, hot shoes into the horn causing burning and thus weakening of the hoof wall.) The iron is bent cold to the shape of the hoof wall and nailed so that the shank comes out about a third of the way up the hoof wall, before the nails are turned over or clenched to keep the shoe in place.

The fitted shoe should be neither too tight nor too loose and the clenched nails should come out in a sloping line parallel with the coronet. The nails have to be well driven home, not placed into old holes and there has to be no gap between the shoe and the underside of the wall. The walls should not be cut down to fit the shoe and the toe has to be rasped properly - that is on the underside and not pared away at the front. The exercise shoe should be a uniform width and thin enough so that in the working horse the frog can take some weight.

In any shod horse the toe has to be trimmed back about 1 cm once a month due to the toe growing faster than the heel. This usually coincides with the shoes being renewed. The horse should walk with a loose free action. If its action is impaired, the trainer should try a different weight shoe since shoe weight can influence a horse's stride.

In the tropics, where there is no road work, the horses can be exercised with racing plates.

Racing Plates

Racing plates are made of an aluminium alloy, weigh around two ounces (50g) and are fitted with some twelve nails as opposed to the seven or eight in the exercise shoes. Aluminium/nickel alloy plates are light, relatively strong and make good racing plates. They have to be strong for if a horse 'spreads a plate' when racing it can cost the horse the race and make it lame. When exercising racehorses in Barbados Bill Marshall fits plates only on the front hooves and leaves the back ones unshod. It is better for the hooves and as the back legs do not carry the same load as the front legs they can be left unshod.

A racing plate has to be as thin and light as possible. It has been estimated that weight carried as plates slows up a racehorse ten times more effectively than the same amount of handicap weight carried in a weight cloth.

In temperate and tropical climates racing plates are fitted to all four hooves two to three days before a race. Racing plates can be left on for two or three races but being light they quickly become damaged.

Clipping

An important part of stablecraft in temperate and tropical climates is clipping.

In winter racehorses produce a thick greasy coat which acts as an excellent protection against wind and rain. The coat, if left in place, would act as a barrier to sweat loss and, if the horse was severely exercised, there would be a good chance that it would overheat. Thus racehorses that are to be worked hard in the winter or all year round in the tropics have to be clipped so as to allow them to sweat freely. Long hair should be clipped as it can become soaked with sweat after work and, besides causing overheating during exercise, on a cold day it can give rise to chills if the horse is not dried and kept warm.

There are a number of different clips for racehorses. A favourite is the 'blanket' clip which leaves unclipped the legs and part of a body that would be covered if a large blanket was thrown over the horse. The only hair left under the imaginary blanket acts as a cushion for the saddle. There is also the 'trace' clip which involves clipping hair only from the belly, flanks and under the neck of the horse.

A clipped, rain-wet horse should always be dried before being put away in the stable. When to clip does depend on the horse but as a rule during the winter months in temperate climates racehorses should be power clipped every six weeks or so. If a horse has a particularly fine coat it should have a blanket clip, otherwise a full clip. Unless the weather becomes very hot rugs are used all the year round in temperate climates and even for exercise in extreme cold. Rugs should not be put on too tightly as they can cause sore withers. If the horse is left standing outside in winter after exercising without a rug, it should be 'rugged up' as soon as possible turning the horse's head in to the wind (to reduce wind resistance) before putting on the rug.

In the tropics racehorses should have a full clip leaving only the forelock, mane and tail long. The mane and tail should be kept thinned by pulling out hairs and not cutting as this only encourages growth. This should be done frequently as pulling too many tail and mane hairs at a time is discomforting for the racehorse.

Calm Racing Stables

Racehorses are subject to stress when they race and when they train. The thoroughbred is a 'highly strung' breed of horse and stabling racehorses singly is both physically and psychologically against the free running herd instincts of horses in the wild. All these factors can make racehorses appear to be 'bored' with their training programme. But it is more complex than this. If they were humans it might be said that they were suffering psychological disorders through a 'stress related confinement'. A good trainer relieves stress by instructing grooms to handle the horse quietly and often grooming is stress relieving and racehorses settle more readily with quiet steady grooms than noisy ones. The grooms should move quietly about the yard and aim to 'upset' the racehorses as little as possible. The less stressed a racehorse the more resistant it is to infection.

Such meticulous attention to detail at the racing stable is required if the trainer is to have success at the race track. A horseshoe nail too near the white line and causing pain, an exercise saddle that pressed too hard on the withers to create an injury, a too noisy groom, an overtight overnight leg bandage, a subclinical viral or bacterial infection from dirty feed or damp stables, bad hay causing indigestion.... the list of possible factors that can bring about failure on the racetrack is endless.

The refined art of stablecraft has to be practiced by the racehorse trainer in order to reduce the probability of racetrack failure. Stablecraft is an essential part of training to win.

CHAPTER SIX

Feeding to Win

"Feed them well".

After one very successful racing season Bill Marshall was asked by a journalist what was his secret to training so many winning racehorses. His reply was; "feed them well".

Diet

The diet of a racehorse is crucial to its ability to perform. In a healthy racehorse which is neither gaining nor losing weight its dietary intake must balance the excretory losses. The chemical components of a horse's diet, the nutrients, can be generally classified as carbohydrates, fats and proteins. Carbohydrates are the main source of a racehorse's energy followed by fats. Under some conditions proteins can supply energy but essentially they build and replace body muscle and general body proteins. Minerals, vitamins and trace elements and water make up the other essential ingredients in a racehorse's diet.

A racehorse is a herbivore and this dictates the structure and function of its digestive system and its food intake. Its favourite diet of grass and other green plants supplies most of these ingredients. The rest, minerals and trace elements, are supplied with the earth the horse eats as it grazes. Stabled racehorses being fed only on oats (for energy and protein) and hay need special vitamin and mineral supplements.

The Digestive System

The horse's digestive system is on a large scale. The total length of the horse's gut from mouth to anus is about 100 feet (30 *m*) and it can hold about 40 gallons (200 *l*) of 'vegetable broth'. The stomach is a relatively small reservoir, holding only around 4 gallons (20 *l*). The small intestine is some 65 feet (20 *m*) and the large intestine is some 25 feet (8 *m*). The salivary glands produce about 10 gallons (40 *l*) of saliva each day and the liver and pancreas around 2 gallons (10 *l*) of digestive fluids each.

A horse takes about three days to completely digest and absorb a meal. Horses almost never vomit although overfeeding can cause the stomach to swell to such an extent that it will rupture. The stomach acts mainly as a reservoir with only a little digestion and some fermentation taking place. There is no absorption of food and the stomach slowly releases the food into the small intestine which is the main digestive region. The small intestine leads into the 'caecum' where parts of the plant food which are difficult to digest - the plant cell walls which are made of cellulose - are broken down by bacteria to carbohydrates. This break down gives off a certain amount of gas which can be heard bubbling through the digestive broth when standing some distance away from the horse.

The carbohydrates, proteins and fats are broken down by special chemicals (enzymes) that are found in the saliva, stomach, liver, pancreas and the small intestine. The enzymes break down large molecules into smaller ones; proteins into amino acids, fats and oils into fatty acids and carbohydrates into simple sugars. These small molecules are absorbed into the blood stream by the small intestine to be used immediately or taken in to stores. The caecum leads into the large intestine which removes most of the water from the food before the damp, indigestible remains are eliminated.

Feed too much and the racehorse will carry too much weight, it will become prone to colic, laminitis, develop skeletal problems and the trainer will waste money on unnecessary food. Feed too little and the horse will first use up its fat supplies and then waste muscle, become lethargic, prone to disease, unable to breed properly and fail to grow at the right rate.

The racehorse is a creature of habit. Digestive juices do not flow and the horse 'goes off its feed' if, for example, it becomes frightened or its environment or feeding times are suddenly changed.

A Balanced Diet

Like all animals the racehorse needs a balanced diet: proteins, carbohydrates, fats, minerals, vitamins and water.

Proteins

Proteins build up muscle and repair and defend the body against attacking organisms. They are made of about 20 different amino acids and the different concentrations of amino acids in proteins give the proteins different characteristics. Too little protein in the diet and the horse starts to break down muscle mass. The protein requirement of young horses is greater than those of adults.

Carbohydrates

Carbohydrates are fuel producing and give the racehorse energy and, as a by-product, heat. Carbohydrates provide the chief source of energy and the chief dietary carbohydrate is starch which is made up of chains of small molecules which are mainly glucose. Starch is found in all cereal grains.

Fats

Fats are also an excellent source of energy, a more 'concentrated ' source of energy than carbohydrates. Fatty acids combine together to give 'triglycerides' which make up much of the horse's dietary fat.

Too much fat and carbohydrate and the racehorse lays down body fat which is only an extra handicap weight to carry in a race. The only way to remove body fat from a horse in training is to exercise more and feed less. Fat can only be burnt off, it cannot be turned into muscle.

Minerals

Minerals are required in varying amounts and perform a number of different functions: for example, calcium and phosphate for bone structure, growth and the absorption of food; iron for the blood and oxygen transport to the muscles; sodium and potassium for correct body fluid composition and nerve and muscle function; copper for skin pigments and iron absorption; iodine for the thyroid gland; magnesium for bone development and muscle function; selenium for muscle function. There is probably a specific requirement for at least twenty different mineral types in a horse. Those needed in high concentrations are calcium (for example the daily calcium requirement is around 20 g), phosphorus, chloride, sodium and potassium. Trace minerals, which are required in lower concentrations but are equally important, include iodine, sulphur, copper, zinc, iron, cobalt and selenium.

Vitamins

Vitamins have a number of essential nutritional roles to play: for example vitamin A helps growth and night vision; vitamin B is also important for growth, the functioning of the nervous system and converting carbohydrates to energy; vitamin D is necessary for the absorption and the utilisation of calcium and phosphate and lack of it will cause rickets and splints; vitamin E is important for the proper functioning of the blood as is vitamin K.

Energy expended in training and maintaining the normal body functions must be met with energy brought into the horse as food. A horse undergoing heavy exercise requires more energy than a horse undergoing light exercise and the best source of energy is carbohydrates and fats. A horse building muscle in training or a growing horse requires more protein (and energy) than a trained or mature one, as does a pregnant mare, and all these requirements can only be supplied via the feed.

The Feed

A wild horse lives off grasslands. Sunshine, wild flowers, weeds and grasses in its natural habitat supply all the horse's nutritional requirements. The stalks and other indigestible parts of the plants supply roughage, 'fibre', to help the food pass through the digestive system. The wild (and domesticated) horse will even eat soil to supply its mineral requirements if they are in short supply, but generally the mixture of plants at different growth cycles supplies a horse with all the essential vitamins and mineral elements. Problems arise when horses are stabled and fed artificial diets.

In the stable a diet of top quality oats and hay will generally meet the racehorse's protein, carbohydrate, fat and fibre requirements but minerals and vitamins have to be fed as supplements. The trainer's problems are: how to obtain good quality oats and hay; to know what quantity of mineral and vitamin supplement to add to the diet; and, most important of all, how much feed to give the horse.

Hay

Hay is rich in protein and minerals like calcium, phosphorous, magnesium and potassium. In a temperate climate like Britain's there are different types of hay which give different protein and mineral yields depending on the plants and when they are cut. Generally the earlier in the year the hay is cut the higher is its protein and mineral content. For example hay made from lucerne (alfalfa), if cut when it is in the half flower stage, can give about 18% of its dry weight in protein and 1.65% of its dry weight in calcium compared to lucerne when cut in full flower where it yields only 15.5% protein and 1.2% calcium. (The absolute values of these percentages obviously depend on many factors which include the species of the plants, the weather and the growing conditions.)

Although lucerne makes the best hay, most hay in Britain, for example, is either meadow or seed. Meadow hay comes from permanent grass fields while seed hay is grown as a rotational crop and contains clover. Seed hay can be a mixture of rye grass and clover or just a mixture of clovers. The protein content of meadow and seed hay (which can equal or be more than the crude protein in oats which is about 11%) is highest when the hay is cut in the early summer. Hay should be cut, dried and stacked within about three days of harvesting and allowed to mature by slight heating in the rick, to be used about five months later. Hay should not be moved once set up in the rick. Mature hay should smell sweet, be greenish, crisp but not too crisp and free from dust.

Cube Feed

Today most trainers feed cube feeds or 'nuts' that are specifically designed for racehorses in training. The protein, fibre and oil content of nuts varies depending on their make, usually around 10% protein and 15% fibre. Although most commercially available brands of racehorse nuts have vitamin and mineral supplements added to them in reasonable proportions, trainers still tend to add their own special favourites. Bill Marshall, for example, adds four extra supplements to the horse's feed. One is a vitamin and iron rich additive which besides vitamins A, D, E, K and B includes the minerals: copper, cobalt, potassium, magnesium, manganese and zinc. He gives a Vitamin E and selenium mixture and a dehydrated seaweed meal which is rich in iodine, chlorophyll and Vitamins A, D and E. An electrolyte supplement is added, which is especially important for training in the tropics where the horses sweat a lot: it contains calcium, phosphate, sodium, chloride and potassium. He also adds a small handful of common salt, sodium chloride, to the feed.

Oats

Best quality oats, like hay, are difficult to find. The oats should be dry and plump with a high flour content which is easily visible as a white powder when they are crushed underfoot. The oat husk should be thin. The oats are best bruised rather than crushed as too much crushing destroys the roughage in the husk and can be very wasteful in terms of spilt flour.

Custom Feeding

As a general rule Bill Marshall feeds a 1000 lb (1 lb = 453.6 gm) racehorse 20 lbs of feed a day. He feeds 10 lbs twice a day and gives a horse a 2:1 weight ratio of two oats (whole or crushed) to one of nuts. The 2:1 ratio of oats and nuts is split equally (10 lbs each feed) between the two feeds and thus a 1000 lb horse theoretically eats about 13 lbs of oats and 7 lbs of nuts each day. He believes that a racehorse should be allowed to eat as much hay as it wishes because 'racehorses will never over-eat hay'. This usually works out to between 10 and 25 lbs of hay per day. But all these feeding weights are arbitrary and depend on each racehorse - some thrive on 15 lbs of oats/nuts feed a day while others need 25 lbs or more.

Racehorses should be fed according to their exercise programme - more work, more feed. They should be fed at the same time each day as this reduces stress and helps prevent indigestion. The general physical state of the animal is an indicator of how many pounds of food to give. The horse's ribs should not be visible but they should be easily felt just under the surface of the skin and there should be no overlying fat pad. The shoulders, withers, neck and tailhead should be examined each day for any thickening and build up of fat.

Mangers

It is best to use removable mangers as they can be taken out of the horse's stable and cleaned. The mangers can also be taken to the feed store where the 'feed man', a vitally important person in any training yard, can make sure that each horse obtains the correct amount of feed and supplements as dictated by the trainer. It is important that mangers are kept off the ground, perhaps hung off the top of the lower stable door. Here the food is not contaminated with horse droppings and wet bedding and bacterial infections from rats and mice are minimised. A manger on the ground also encourages a race-horse to develop the bad habit of eating its own droppings and bedding.

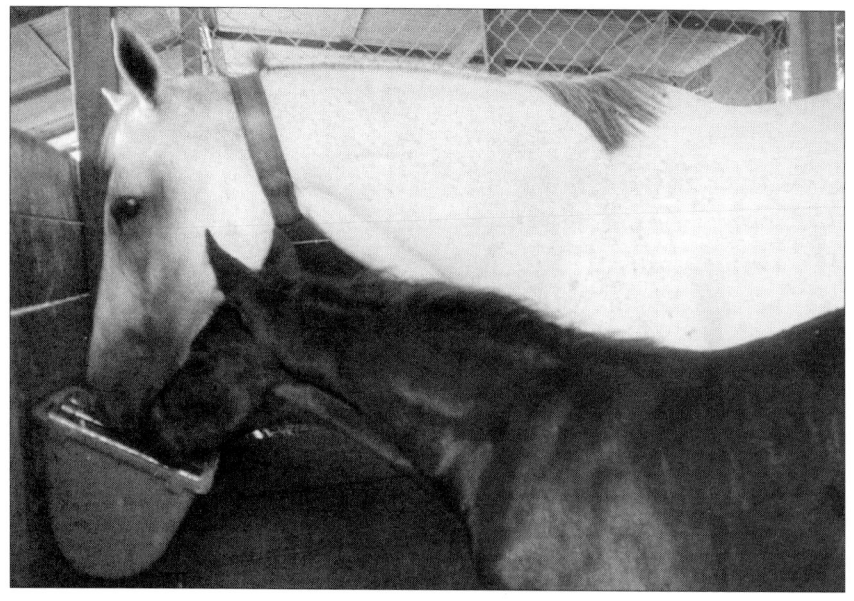

Removable mangers.

Diet and Droppings

The trainer should always examine the horse's droppings as a way of assessing health and its ability to digest its food. The droppings should be dark-lemon coloured balls that easily break up. It is a sign of indigestion if the droppings are hard, streaked with mucus or there are whole oats in them, perhaps due to not enough fibre in the diet because the horse is not eating sufficient quantities of hay. Droppings with whole oats in them can also mean there is trouble with the teeth–especially the molars - that grind up the food. The trainer should keep a look out for red and white worms in the dung and immediately call the vet if there is any sign of blood.

Bran Mash

In temperate climates, providing the horse is not racing, Bill Marshall believes that racehorses benefit from a linseed oil/bran mash twice a week. The mash is fattening but gives the racehorse's coat a fine gloss and it also acts as a mild laxative. To make a mash the linseeds are soaked in cold water for at least 24 hours before use to soften them and remove any toxins. A pound of soaked seeds is added to a gallon bucket of water and the mixture brought to the boil. It is simmered for about 20 minutes stirring all the while to stop the seeds from burning. The seeds burst to produce a thick, sticky jelly. Bran is added in the ratio of one linseed to two brans and then the mash is left to stand for four to five hours. A big scoopful of the mash is added to the feed and racehorses love it.

Grass

Racehorses should be allowed to nibble at grass whenever they can. 'Dr Field Grass' or 'Dr Green' is considered by many trainers to be 'a curer of many evils'.

Water and Sweating

Horses need water to digest their oats, nuts, grass and hay and to replace water lost as sweat. Water should be freely given and kept in a large, removable, heavy duty plastic or galvanised bucket. The advantage of removable buckets is that they are easily cleaned and refilled at a single source. Racehorses will self-regulate their water intake and if water is always available they will not over drink. Over drinking can lead to colic.

It is important to use the same water supply each day - some horses will refuse to drink if there is an abrupt change in the taste of the water. Also horses will refuse to drink if the water becomes too cold. It is not correct, as some 'horse people' believe, that horses should not be given water when they are too hot or after strenuous work. In fact this is the time when their water intake has to be increased to replace that lost from exercise or sweating.

Water intake is an important aspect of stabling, especially in the tropics where it is estimated that a horse may need as much as 60 litres of water a day. It is useful to add salt to the food or water of exercising horses to help replace those electrolytes, mainly sodium and potassium chloride, lost through sweating. A litre of horse sweat contains about eight grams of sodium chloride and two grams of potassium chloride. Some 70% of the body weight of the racehorse comes from water and the degree of dehydration can be roughly assessed by the colour of the urine. The paler the urine the less the dehydration. Horses urinate several times each day and usually when they are in their stables over their bedding. They seem to prefer to urinate over absorbent ground - perhaps to avoid splashing their legs.

Some heat is lost when horses urinate, but most heat is lost through sweating. Sweating is essential to prevent racehorses from overheating when they work.

Sweating and Shivering

The skin plays a vital role in maintaining the health of the racehorse. It is composed of three layers. An outer layer (epidermis) contains mainly dead cells that are being produced by the innermost layer and are continuously being sloughed off. The next much thicker layer (the dermis) contains blood vessels, nerves, collagen - a fibrous connective tissue which helps 'bind' the dermis together oil (sebaceous) and sweat (apocrine) glands and the hair follicles which produce the hairs which lie in a sheath or an infolding of the outer layer. The sweat and oil glands secrete into the hair sheath. Horses sweat through large numbers of sweat glands that are associated with the hairs and sweating is stimulated by the 'flight or fight' hormone adrenalin which is carried to the glands via the blood stream. The sweat glands extract the liquid from the small blood vessels, the capillaries, that lie just below the surface of the skin. In winter a horse that is not clipped produces a thick coat which is covered with oil or grease from the sebaceous glands and this 'waxy' covering acts as an excellent protective covering against wind and rain.

The horse sweats when it becomes hot during exercise or hot weather and the skin is cooled as the sweat evaporates due to the energy required to turn the liquid water into a gas (the latent heat of evaporation).

The third layer of the skin (subcutis) is fatty and contains muscle fibres which can move the skin and bring about shivering. The skin also reduces heat loss by raising the hair follicles to trap a layer of warm air and by muscle fibres releasing heat during shivering from the process of muscle contraction.

Dry–Coat

Racehorses sometimes lose their ability to sweat. At first they seem to be over-sweating and this is followed by an inability to sweat at all. To remove body heat the horses pant just like very hot dogs. The horse's skin becomes hard and the condition is known as dry–coat. It can occur in temperate climates and might be stress related. Dry–coat is not related to water intake.

In the tropics dry–coat is much more dangerous. Exercising horses can dramatically overheat and, in extreme cases, die. The only cure is rest, ideally in a cooler climate. Bill Marshall once knew of an Indian vet who: "would solve all his cases of dry-coat by packing the racehorses off to the hills for three to four months. They always started to sweat again once they came down to the lowlands. In Barbados I now send a horse with dry-coat up to a stud farm where it can be cooled by the trade wind breezes. It's like going to the Indian hills".

CHAPTER SIX — *The Art & Science of Racehorse Training*

CHAPTER SEVEN

Buying and Breaking

A future Derby winner?

In the previous chapters some of the important scientific basics of training and the art and science of stabling and feeding a racehorse were dealt with. This chapter is concerned with the collection of skills that a trainer needs to buy and to break in a (young) racehorse and prepare it for a regime of strenuous exercises that is custom designed to bring the horse to its performance peak on race day.

The Yearlings

The age of a racehorse is, even though it may be born some six months into the year, always set from January 1st in the year in which it was born. Horses are foals until the next January 1st when they become yearlings. Thus yearlings are colts, fillies or geldings (castrated males) aged between one and two years.

The Young Racehorse

Today much of the big money in horse racing is won by young racehorses, two or three year old colts and fillies, winning flat races like, for example, the British Classic races. The enormous costs of breeding and purchasing these young horses means that, in order to recoup some of their owners' capital outlay, many of these successful horses are retired by the time they are four year olds. Owners are often reluctant to run a successful colt as a four year old, especially in weight for age races, in case it is beaten and its value depreciated. It is almost a rule nowadays that a three year old British Classic winner, if a stallion, will be retired to stud so that as a four year old its owners can pick up the large stud fees.

Horses destined for these short, flat racing careers are usually sold as yearlings at prestigious sales held in Europe and America. Horses racing over the hurdles or fences do not start their careers until they are three (for hurdles) or four years old (for fences), often first starting out as flat racing horses.

The Sales

Depending on the breeder but usually around July or August the yearlings are brought in from the paddocks and their night roamings are over. They are walked for about an hour each day being led on by a head collar and in some breeder's yards prior to the sales the yearlings will be lunged - that is sent round in right and left-handed circles on long single reins that are attached to bitless bridles.

The buying season for yearlings opens in July at Keeneland, Kentucky, America and ends in Newmarket, England in December. At the sale rings, which are auctions, owners, trainers, bloodstock agents and syndicates bid fabulous prices for the untried yearlings. In 1985 Robert Sangster and the Irish trainer Vincent O'Brien paid $13.1 million at the Keeneland sales for a yearling. Two years earlier Sheik Mohammed al Maktoum paid over $10.2 million for *Snaafi Dancer* which turned out to be useless as a two year old and was never raced at a race course.

Britain's most prestigious sale, the Tattersalls Highflyer Sales, now called the Houghton Yearling Sales, are held every year in Newmarket in late September or early October. The Newmarket based auctioneering firm, Tattersalls, was first created in the eighteenth century by Richard Tattersall who, in 1776, founded a business to sell horses and hounds at Hyde Park Corner, London. The family specialised in thoroughbred horses and Tattersalls was a family owned business until the middle of this century. The family moved from London to Newmarket and developed their thoroughbred sales in their Park Paddocks yard.

Today breeders have to have their applications to enter Tattersalls (Highflyer) Houghton Yearling Sales by March and demand always far exceeds the number of lots that the auctioneers allocate to the sales. Tattersalls sends out travelling assessors to each of the breeders and, after assessing the pedigree and potential of all the yearlings, by mid summer the 350 top yearlings are selected.

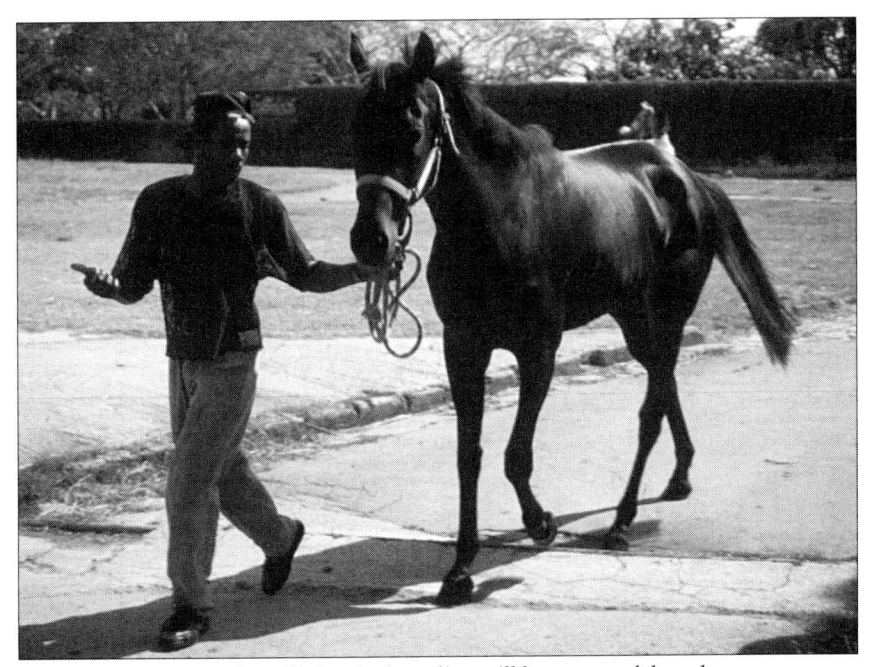

There is no guarantee that a high priced yearling will be a successful racehorse.

CHAPTER SEVEN — *The Art & Science of Racehorse Training*

The horses arrive two or three days before the sales and are examined by the trainers, would be owners and their vets. It is quite possible for a well bred yearling to be pulled out of a box as many as 40 times a day. The yearlings are walked out of their stables, the grooms parade the horses up and down and the trainers feel the ligaments and tendons behind their fore and hind legs - a ritual that is as much part of the trainer's life as the morning gallops. Most yearlings come to the sales with a 'wind certificate' which should have been signed within the prior three weeks of their arrival. All thoroughbred auctions are based on 'what you see is what you get'; however under special circumstances (which involves examination of the horse by a panel of vets) if the purchaser is unhappy that the yearling is 'not sound in the wind' it is possible to declare the sale void.

Form and Lineage

Probably the most important factors in determining the price obtained for a horse at a sale is the horse's pedigree - its lineage.

The English Thoroughbred was the result of a selected breeding programme that lasted about a hundred years from 1650 until around 1750. The modern thoroughbred evolved from crosses between horses from Arabia and nearby countries and mixed English breeds. (It is larger than an Arab and faster over middle distances.) These horses were crossed at some time in the seventeenth century and three particular stallions - the Godolphin Arabian, the Darley Arabian and the Byerley Turk - are considered to be important members of the gene pool of the modern male racehorse.

The Godolphin Arabian was born in 1724 and in one version of its origins it is said to have been discovered in Paris working as a carthorse! Another version was that the King of France was presented with the Arab by the Bey of Tunis who had originally obtained the horse from Yemen for his stud. Lord Godolphin purchased the Godolphin Arabian from an Edward Coke of Longford Hall in Derbyshire who, supposedly, first brought the horse to England from France.

The Darley Arabian was born in 1700 in Syria. It was obtained by Thomas Darley the British Consul and sent back to England to the family seat at Aldby in East Yorkshire. *Flying Childers*, one of the early famous racehorses, was sired by the Darley Arabian.

The Byerley Turk was obtained as war booty from the Turks by Captain Byerley after their defeat at Buda in 1686. He used the horse on later campaigns including the Battle of the Boyne in 1690 before sending it out to stud in County Durham and later to Goldsborough Hall near York.

For some time the dam's side of the development of the thoroughbred racehorse was ignored until some important research was published at the end of the nineteenth century (see Craig, Chapter V The Dam, Lines and Leading Brood-mares, for more details). Before then only the sire lines had been considered but, obviously, both dam and sire are equally important in the genetic makeup of an offspring.

In Britain racehorse form and lineage have been continuously recorded for over two hundred years. In the eighteenth century 'Calendars' of race results were regularly produced and as early as 1679 Nelson's Register recorded 'horse matches'. At first recordings were not very accurate but the standards were set when James Weatherby, the then Keeper of the Match Book for the Jockey Club, published a racing Calendar in 1773 and today this publication is Britain's official racing calendar.

In 1791 'An Introduction to a General Stud Book' was also published by James Weatherby and it was probably his nephew who published the 'General Stud Book' in 1813 which became the accepted standard record of a racehorse's pedigrees. Armed with a Weatherby Calendar and General Stud Book a potential buyer can theoretically trace both the breeding and performance record of any horse over 150 years of its ancestry. Today Weatherbys' acts as a data base to the racing world and the latest pedigree and performance information on almost any racehorse can be obtained from Weatherby's computers.

The Tattersalls (Highflyer) Houghton Sales catalogue gives the racing careers of the three previous generations of a yearling - both the sires and the dams. In the mid 1980s a number of yearlings went for over £1 million each and in 1988 the top selling yearling at the Tattersalls Highflyer Sales fetched 2.4 million guineas (a guinea is a former British gold coin now worth £1.05p). A well bred colt yearling can be a worth-

CHAPTER SEVEN

The Art & Science of Racehorse Training

while investment - a three year old racehorse with a superb flat racing career and an excellent pedigree could fetch £20 million before he is put out to stud.

Although the thoroughbred is an accepted breed the outcome of any thoroughbred match is never certain. Thus all top class yearling sales are expensive gambles because inheritance equally depends on the female and male line and, as was the case of *Snaafi Dancer*, there is absolutely no guarantee that sire line's ability will be directly inherited.

Buying a Yearling

Although many equine scientists are looking for ways in which future racing performance can be directly correlated with a yearling's pedigree, to date they have had little or no success. Nevertheless a yearling's pedigree is the most important criterion in deciding its value, providing it is 'sound', has a good general shape or 'conformation' and is a good 'character'. It is probable that horses bred 'in the purple' from famous, race-winning parents, grandparents and great grandparents have, statistically, a much better chance of producing offspring that will run faster than those with a more ordinary lineage but it is by no means certain that they will.

The Sale Room: Tattersalls Highflyer Yearling sales.

Soundness

Scientific methods are more successful when they are employed to measure the 'soundness' of a yearling. X-rays give good evidence of bone damage or skeletal deformities. Electrocardiography and echocardiography can not only be used to look for heart deformities before the yearling is bought but also to estimate heart size. There is some correlation between a large heart size and above average racing performance.

Wind

The yearling's 'wind' has to be sound with a regular, easy breathing pattern. Any noise in breathing when the horse is at rest or when it comes out of its stable probably means that there is a fault in the respiratory system. In the worst case there can be severe paralysis of the voice box or even tumours. Other danger signs of a malfunctioning respiratory system are widened nostrils, pushing out of the head as the horse breathes in, and a non relaxed 'double breathing' out which is known as 'broken wind'.

The soundness of the upper airways can be examined using recently invented fibre optic endoscopes that are introduced via the nose into the voice box and trachea of the horse but, naturally enough, many vendors are wary of allowing yearlings to be 'scoped'.

Conformation

The purchase is also made on the 'conformation' or shape of the yearling, but 'good conformation' is often a matter of personal preference as there are no set scientific rules for conformation. Bill Marshall believes that, as a general rule, a young racehorse should have a good length from shoulder to buttocks, a strong looking neck and ideally a deep girth and loins. A strong back, high withers, wide gaskins, straight hocks and above all that almost indefinable quality in a horse - everything should be in balance. The horse's limbs should work in parallel and conditions known as 'outbowed', 'cow hocked' or 'closed in front' are definitely to be avoided (see page 157). The yearling should stand square on its four legs - if it is lifting a foreleg there is something wrong.

The way in which the yearling comes out of the stable is also important. It should come out alert, bright eyed with a bouncy, easy action, and its legs should work in parallel.

Character
Finally it is important to have some idea of the 'character' of the yearling and, when possible, the potential purchaser should talk to its groom. A brave and competitive racehorse is best; highly strung is all right; a cowardly, sulky or lazy animal should be avoided. Some thoroughbreds are bad-tempered, others are stubborn, all are easily frightened.

Breaking In

The training of a young flat or jump racehorse starts as soon as it reaches the racing stables. Most thoroughbreds destined for the flat racing course go to the flat trainer's yard as yearlings. At one time there were attempts to race yearlings but this has long been banned and yearlings are never ridden. It's the flat trainer's job to break them in and turn them into winning two year olds. Breaking in any racehorse is a real art and the trainer uses calmness, kindness and gentleness. This applies as much to a yearling as it does to a four year old and 'rodeo style' bucking and rearing around a field is not the way in which to break in a horse.

Throughout the autumn, in Britain, the yearlings start to arrive at the flat trainer's stables. The horses come from stud farm and sales in Britain, Ireland, France, Germany and America and from other trainers' yards. By early December the wheeling and the dealing is over and the yearlings are in their trainer's stables and ready for breaking in.

The First Few Months
As soon as the yearlings arrive their parentage is checked. This may be carried out by a number of different methods. In some countries the yearlings are given a mouth tattoo to mark their parentage. Or if there is any serious doubt, parentage can be checked by an analysis of the yearling's blood type. Blood typing is the most reliable method of

control (it is similar to finger printing in man) and in Britain since 1986 it has been compulsory for a foal to have its blood type recorded before it can be registered in the General Stud Book. The yearling's parentage can easily be checked providing the parents were blood typed.

The Break In

In Britain, for example, the flat season closes in November with the November Handicap at Doncaster being the last 'big' race of the season. Flat racing does not start until March, again usually at Doncaster, so the British trainer has to 'break in' and prepare the yearlings that arrived in the autumn for the start of the season as two year olds in the following spring. But not all the yearlings will be ready to race as two year olds by March: that depends on how well they develop physically and under the training programme.

Breaking and Exercise Bits

The first move when breaking in a horse is to introduce a breaking bit into its mouth, which is usually a bit consisting of a single wide stainless steel bar, the mouthpiece, loosely connected to a ring at either end. A good breaking bit is one with a few loose keys attached to the bar. It is important that horses do not become 'dry-mouthed' and the keys give the horse something to play with to produce a steady stream of saliva. The yearling 'accepts the bit' when it relaxes its jaw and opens its mouth to receive it.

The racehorse is never controlled by force alone and has to be trained to obey its rider's signals which, in part, are transmitted through the bit. The bit should be seen as an extension of the rider's hands and young racehorses should never be allowed to become frightened of the bit. Most racehorse trainers use 'snaffle' bits on broken in horses which act on the corner of the thoroughbred's mouth and on the 'bars' of the mouth (the toothless gums between the front and back teeth). The mouthpiece of the snaffle bit may be made of a light alloy, aluminium, stainless steel or even a thick rubber bar as in a 'loose ring mullen mouth snaffle'. The character of the horse usually dictates the type of bit used by the trainer. 'Soft mouthed' horses, which do not pull and are easily controlled, might need only a solid rubber mouthpiece while headstrong, 'hard mouthed' horses, which pull hard on their bit, may need to be controlled by employing specially jointed mouthpieces so that tension on the reins causes the two parts of the bit to act like a nutcracker on the sides of the mouth.

Snaffle bits slide up the mouth and the racehorse then tends to hold its head in a straight line with the neck. All racehorses are encouraged during training to take 'hold of the bit', which is not the case when training ordinary horses. The horse will even 'lean on the bit' when an unbalanced jockey struggles to maintain his balance.

Long Reins

Once the yearling can take a bit in its mouth it is then steered from behind with ten foot long reins attached to the side rings. Everything is done slowly. The horse is walked and turned, walked and turned, first left and then right until it becomes accustomed to the idea of pressure and direction from the bit and the rein acting from behind. This job is usually carried out by stable 'lads' who are responsible for breaking in the yearlings every autumn.

The Lungeing Rein

The modern thoroughbred is a racing machine that has been bred to run. On a lunge a young racehorse will physically extend itself to such an extent that, without realising, it can seriously damage its back, muscles, ligaments and tendons. A young two year old's back can even be damaged by trotting too fast. Bill Marshall is one trainer who never trains with a lungeing rein believing that on the lunge the young horse can move too quickly and damage its back.

Saddling-Up

It is essential to build the young horse's confidence with the bit and rein before attempting to saddle up. The saddle and girth are put on in a large loose box and the girth tightened until the horse just feels it. Then the saddled horse with head collar and reins is walked round in the box in both directions and then led outside the box and walked again. This is repeated on the following day but this time the horse is walked, if possible, outside the box with the saddle, girth and long reins.

When the horse is accustomed to saddle, girth and reins it is time to mount it. Whilst the saddled horse is being led round in the loose box, the handler leans against its flanks. As soon as the horse is used to being leant against, a rider should lie across its back while a second person continues to lead it round the box. This is repeated on the following day. If the rider lies over the horse's back while it is moving the horse is less likely to tense up; trying to move a tense, stationary horse can cause the horse to buck. When the moving horse accepts the person on its back it is time for the rider to sit up, while all the time the horse is being walked round the box. The reins are gathered, the horse walked both ways round the box and if it doesn't buck it can be led out of the box.

First Rides

It is essential that a newly broken in horse is walked 'in balance'. Bill Marshall describes this as follows: "The back legs carry the weight of the rider and the reins are held gently, with the horse tucking its nose in. Using his legs the rider should gently kick the thoroughbred into a walk. Only a very gentle pressure on the reins should be applied to pull the horse up. For a few days the horse should be walked for about an hour a day using a tight, 'unslouched' walk with the aim of using as many of the yearling's muscles as possible to increase general skeletal muscle tone.

After walking for a few days, and if the horse appears relaxed and unafraid it can be trotted. Once again everything is done calmly and gently. When trotting I insist that the yearling should not be allowed to 'reach forward' but should move with his head tucked back thus performing what I call a 'collected trot' with short high steps, a shortened back and a lowered rump. Horses ridden on too loose a rein will lower their heads and 'slop along'.

Horses can be collected at any speed, even at a gallop, and young racehorses have to be collected which strengthens the horses back and brings the hind legs under the horse. It is also important never to allow a young racehorse to trot or canter up a road too fast. The hard road surface could do irreparable damage to muscles, tendons and developing bone.

Trotting and Cantering - Turning and Leading

After about a fortnight when the young racehorse has become used to being walked and trotted it is now schooled to turn. The horse is first trotted in figures of eight with the work rider moving from a sitting to a rising trot but taking care in the rising trot to rise and sit gently so as to avoid banging the horse's back. The rider should never use a slack rein but must make sure that the head is only in light contact.

The horse is then taught to canter gently round the figure of eight with the rider standing 'jockey style' in the stirrups. The horse learns to turn with a rhythm and to lead with its right leg when turning to the right and left when turning to the left. The work rider rides forward and moves his shoulders to swing the horse on to the correct leg. A good rider puts a horse on to the correct leg for a turn without giving the leading a thought.

Work Riders

Work riders are very important in training - if the horse is good trainers can always get a good jockey but good work riders are often hard to find. A good work rider is one who keeps the horse 'in balance' and does not pull on the mouth or the head of the horse. A very important rule in training is to leave a horse's mouth and head alone as much as possible; racehorses should have firm responsive mouths.

The shortest distance between two points is a straight line so it is important that the work rider teaches the young horse to canter in a straight line as soon as possible.

Balance and Control

A yearling or young two year old is in the most rapid growth phase of its life and the trainer must never forget this. The back and limb muscles, tendons and ligaments are all unaccustomed to the rider's weight and everything has to be taken steadily. The horse has to be collected and in balance so that it can unleash the power in its back legs when required by the work rider or jockey. 'Balance' is extremely important in riding a horse and it means that the horse should always be allowed to be in charge of its own activities. A good work rider or jockey will instinctively keep the mount in balance so that it is not 'falling over its own legs' and its centre of gravity is in the right place.

Because of the extra weight of the neck and head the horse's centre of gravity lies more towards its fore than its hind legs. Thus the horses 'natural balance' tends to put more weight on the front of the horse which in a moving horse causes the front legs to hit the ground hard while the more powerful driving muscles of the hind end are acting less efficiently. In a collected horse, the nose is brought in and back, and the hind quarters are dropped with the result that the centre of gravity moves back and more weight is carried over the hind legs. This improves the efficiency of the drive from the hind legs and, if the horse is ridden like this from the start, the rump will develop greater muscle bulk and the horse's natural balance will thus also improve.

Breaking in Difficult Horses

Breaking in, the first ridden walks and trots, all require patience and calm and nothing must be rushed. If there are no hitches the horse is broken in within a month. But all horses are different. Some take longer to learn and some are more highly spirited than others.

The same techniques described above can be used for breaking in any age of horse but there are some tricks with difficult horses. Bill Marshall remembers "a three year old filly, highly strung and out of the purple, and no one could get near her with any exercise tack". He was bet a dozen bottles of champagne by some members of the sporting press that the filly couldn't be broken in. He went to her stable holding the head collar and as soon as he walked inside the box she flew at him. Head down and teeth bared. He hit her hard with the collar and she pulled back. Bill Marshall: "That filly was wild but I had a trick up my sleeve. If you take any horse that is impossible to break in to a strange place at night and in the pitch dark you can do anything with it. I did that with the filly and had no trouble tacking her up. The next day after a small feed and a walk up and down the yard with the tack on I trotted her on Newmarket Heath: much to the amazement of the press. I enjoyed the champagne!"

Disciplining Young (and old) Horses

It is important that racehorses learn 'good manners' and some have to be disciplined. A good trainer will almost never strike a horse but if the trainer has to, the disciplined horse has to immediately connect pain with the punishable action. Hitting a horse for throwing a rider after the rider is on the floor is too late; likewise striking the horse a minute after it has tried to savage someone is also too late. Striking the horse in either case will only cause it to be confused. To be of any use the punishment blow has to be struck within seconds of the horse's actions that are to be prevented.

It is an important point that punishment is generally only helpful in trying to prevent an action and that it is of little use in forcing racehorses to do something.

The Three Basic Rules of Training

It can be seen that the first rule of training is to be kind and gentle with the horses in the trainer's charge and the trainer should avoid, whenever possible, striking a horse.

It can be argued that the second and third important rules of training are that the trainer must never lose his or her temper with a horse and that the trainer should never be scared of a horse - or at least not show fear. A horse will quickly pick up any sign of fear.

Plate 1

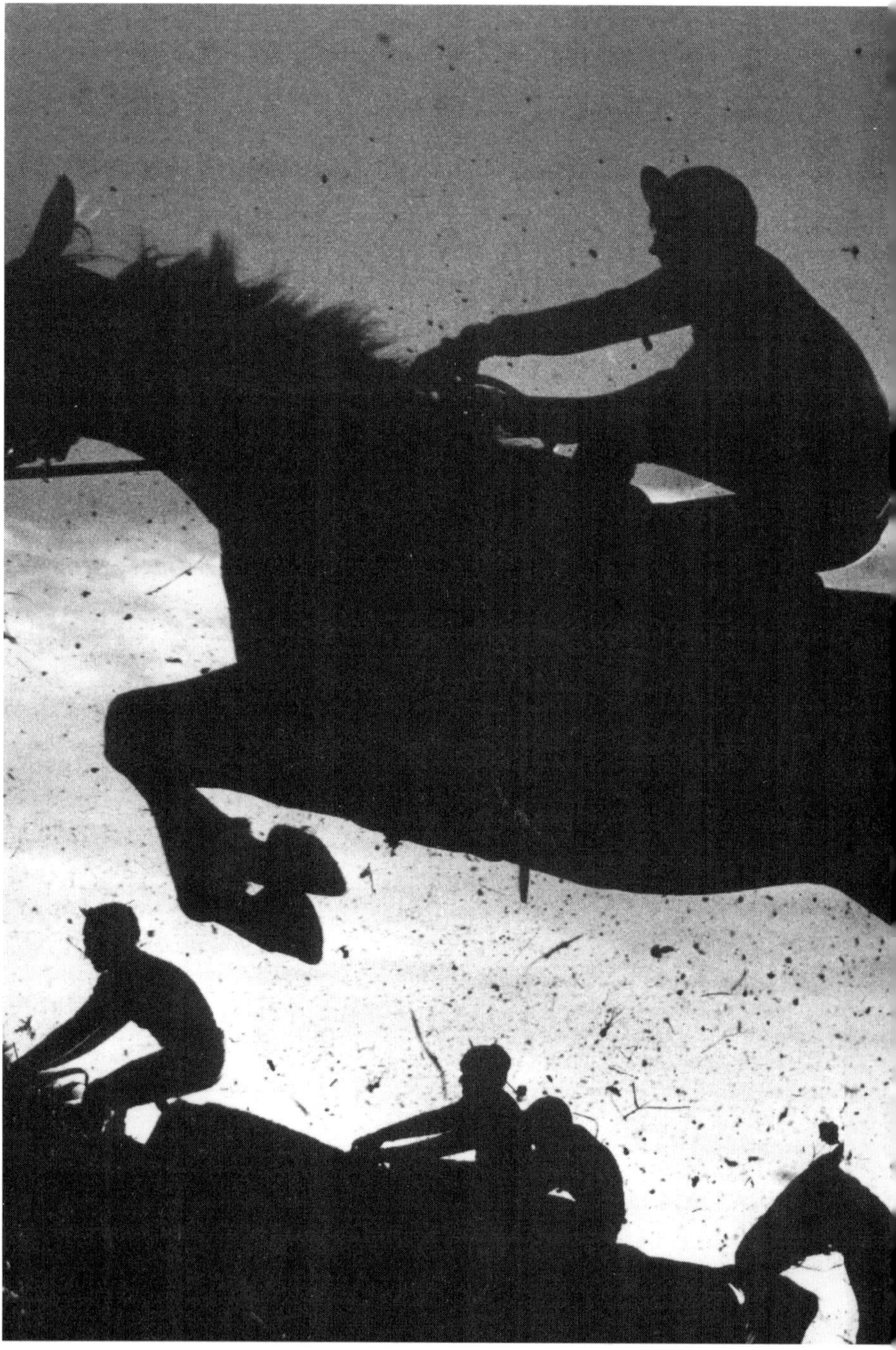

Plate 2

Plate 3

CHAPTER EIGHT

Flat Race Training: the Routine

Racehorses should always be worked alongside each other in groups.

In well run racing stables much of life is routine. Racehorses like routine and quickly become attuned to the daily cycle of chores that are part of any trainer's life. It is not long before new arrivals start to look forward to their regular outings to the exercise track. Routine is important in any training yard as thoroughbreds are an excitable breed of horse and once they know their daily routines they are easier to manage and train. The routine is much the same in flat or jump racing stables, although there are two differences: jump horses are usually older than flat racers and they have to be schooled to jump.

CHAPTER EIGHT *The Art & Science of Racehorse Training*

In any racing stables, tropical and temperate, flat or jump, the day always begins with the stable grooms or 'lads', men or women who look after the horses, checking that the horses in their care ate up their previous day's feed; that they did not hurt themselves during the night and that the horses are generally in good condition for the day's exercise. Then the lads clean or muck out the stables and tack up the horses.

Tropical Routines

In both tropical and temperate climates the daily routine in the yard and on the exercise tracks is much the same: early morning feed; muck out; brush over; tack-up; warm-up; exercise; warm-down; wash and light brush-down; lunch; rest; thorough grooming; evening stables; prepare bedding; second feed.

In the tropics there is an exception in that the horses are fed after morning training so as to give the horses more time to exercise in the cool part of the day. Feeding after exercise does not appear to affect training or race track performance.

In Bill Marshall's flat training yard in Barbados, the head lad arrives around 5.15 each morning while it is still dark and unlocks the doors to the yard and tack room. Bill Marshall arrives around 5.25 and, just as the sun is about to rise, he discusses the day's exercise programme with the head lad and starts handing out the leg bandages and exercise tack. It is not long before the tacked up horses are clattering round the yard on their first walk of the day. During this warm up period all the horses are led through an old set of starting gates so that they lose their fear of the gates. The younger horses reluctantly allow themselves to be led through the stalls, the older horses saunter through without fear. In the tropics, warm up lasts for about three quarters of an hour and the exercise period is limited to the first few cool hours of daylight - from 6am to 8am in Barbados. The horses receive their first feed after morning exercise at around 9am.

Number of Feeds

Some racing stables feed the horses five times a day both in the tropics and in temperate climates but as long as hay is given ad-lib two feeds are just as effective and are easier on the yard staff to give than five. The advantage of ad-lib hay is that the horses' stomach tends always to be partly full (as for example when they are frequently eating grass 'on the plains' in their natural wild state) and nibbling at the hay also helps relieve confinement stress - the horses have something to do all day: munch and nibble hay.

In tropical and temperate climates the second feed can be given after evening/afternoon stables, which is usually around 4.30pm, after the trainer has inspected the horses.

Warming Up and Down

One advantage of having the exercise track or gallops some distance from the stables is that the horses are warmed up on the way to the exercise grounds, otherwise horses have to be walked by their grooms. In the Caribbean Bill Marshall uses 'work riders' to trot, canter and gallop the horses as the 'lads' only groom, tack up and lead the horses. In Britain grooms often work the horses on the exercise track. The Caribbean grooms even pay young men or 'hot walkers' out of their wages to rapid walk the horses before and after exercise.

Racehorses can 'over heat' in the tropics so it is doubly important that they are walked rapidly for at least three quarters of an hour before (to warm them up) and after (to warm them down) exercise. After exercise the horses are first warmed down by fast walking until they have stopped breathing heavily and then gently hosed or bucketed down to remove all the sweat and dust of exercise. Washing down should be gentle, for 'hot muscles' can seize up if buckets of cold water are thrown over them straight away after intense exercise. After washing down the excess fresh water is removed with a metal sweat scraper. Then the horses are thoroughly dried with a cloth and rapid walked again before they are returned to their stables and given their first feed of the day.

Swimming

If the racing stables is near the coast one great advantage of training in the tropics is that the horses can be exercised by swimming in warm sea water. This is especially beneficial to horses with cut legs as the salt

CHAPTER EIGHT   *The Art & Science of Racehorse Training*

Washing down after exercise in the tropics.

water rapidly cleans and heals nicks and scratches. The tropical salt water also appears to strengthen tendons, although it is unclear why as the skin is an impermeable barrier.

Most thoroughbreds love to swim in warm sea water. Bill Marshall recalls that one of his racehorses, *Great Bliss*, became a 'swimming fanatic'. *Great Bliss's* stable lad could swim well and most mornings racehorse and lad would set off through the surf together. In Barbados there is usually a heavy, breaking inshore swell. Because of the large waves the horse, which set a fast pace, would soon be lost from view even though they were not far from the shore. *Great Bliss* always returned, groom in tow, both 'blowing' hard from battling against the breakers.

Swimming exercise, especially in the open sea, is very strenuous exercise. Racehorses can be kept in top condition and raced more often since this type of exercise is less of a strain on their legs than conventional track exercise.

Bill Marshall rarely swam horses in Britain believing that the circular swimming pools, for example the one at Newmarket, are always too cold; that fresh water is not particularly good for the horses' legs and that horses soon became bored swimming round in circles. He also believed that the degree of boredom suffered by a racehorse attached to the rotating arms of 'mechanical horse walkers' far outweighed any training advantage the horse received as they were sent round in apparently never-ending circles.

Training in Temperate Climates

The fundamental racehorse training technique, which applies equally to thoroughbred training for flat or jump racing in temperate and tropical climates, is essentially concerned with gradually building up the racehorse to its peak performance through a training schedule that can be divided up into three main categories: conditioning, slow steady exercise and fast work. This build up takes time, patience and routine.

By February, in Britain for example, all the two year olds are more or less broken in and ready to begin a programme of steady exercise. Bill Marshall's training system (as with many other modern day trainer's) is based on 'lots' and the two year olds enter the system in the third lot (see below). The first few months of the new year are the time when these young two year olds are most physically vulnerable - a slip on the ice in the yard and down could go thousands, perhaps millions, of dollars. The man responsible to the trainer for an ice free yard and the daily running of the stables is the 'head lad'.

The Head Lad

The head lad is in charge of all the other grooms, and it is his job to ensure that the stabled horses are kept calm, settled, and that the other grooms do not unnecessarily disturb the horses.

Each groom is responsible for two or three horses and the head lad is directly responsible to the trainer. Head lads like trainers easily work a 60 hour week. The head lad accompanies the trainer on evening rounds and usually bandages up the horses' legs.

The Daily Routine

In Britain in a flat (and jump) racing yard the trainer's day starts early. In the high northern latitudes the trainer never has to worry about the day becoming too hot for exercising - early mornings in a British winter, autumn or early spring are usually cold, dark and damp!

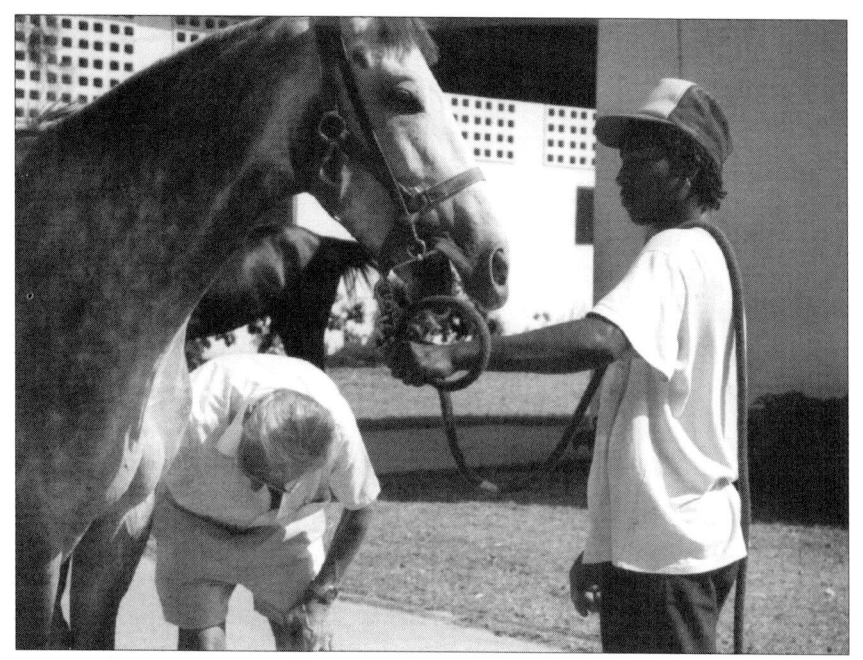

CHAPTER EIGHT   *The Art & Science of Racehorse Training*

Feeling the horse's leg: an essential part of the daily routine.

In winter the grooms arrive at the yard about an hour before daylight and in summer around 5.45. After checking their horses they feed them. The horses are fed before exercise (unlike the tropics) and the horses are normally groomed, tacked up, walked, trotted and sometimes cantered by the grooms.

Tacking Up

The grooms obtain the exercise tack from the tack room, under the eye of the trainer or head lad. The exercise saddle is fitted over a saddle cloth and a thick exercise sponge which has the important role of protecting and cushioning the horse's back during exercises. Bill Marshall uses a breast-plate to prevent the saddle slipping back and a single bridle but never uses nose bands or martingales believing that they do not perform any useful function.

All the bandages are kept in the tack room and cleaned and rolled after use. Exercise bandages are usually stockinette, slightly-elastic polo bandages which are wound round the forelegs on horses that have a habit of clipping themselves with their back hooves to leave small bumps or nicks and cuts. Bandages are also used on the hind legs to protect any nicks and cuts caused during exercise by other horses' hooves.

The Lot System

While the horses are being fed, mucked out, brushed over and tacked up by the stable grooms a trainer who uses the lot system might match available riders with horses and set up the 'lots'. Training using the system of lots means dividing up the horses into three or more lots which are further subdivided in to groups.

First Lot

First lot is a lot made up of racehorses for fast work; it is for the fittest horses and some of them could be racing in a week's time. They are always exercised before the other two lots and are worked hard on the gallops, usually on a Wednesday and Saturday. Gallop days are known as 'work days' and first lot horses soon learn when it is a work day, coming out of their stables full of energy.

Second Lot

This lot is for steady, slow work, cantering, and these horses are not galloped.

Third Lot

In this lot the emphasis is on conditioning and a gradual build up or work. Two year olds, horses just coming into training and lame or sick horses returning to training are worked steadily in this lot. It is important to bring a horse into good condition by walking and trotting in lot three before exposing it to lot two exercise regimes.

Work Days

After the list of horses for the three or more lots is made up it is passed to the head groom. If it is a work day - a Wednesday or a Saturday - the trainer should inspect the gallops before first lot arrives. This is important as the 'gallop man', who prepares the gallops, could have failed to fill in a hole or moles might have been at work during the night - one bad stumble on the gallops and a torn tendon or ligament could mean the end of a great horse. A good maxim for any trainer is that 'thoroughbreds are at risk with every stride they take'.

The ideal situation for any trainer is to have two exercise tracks - one track for galloping and the other for trotting and cantering. Because of the climate and the easier maintenance many British trainers use 'all weather' canters and gallops which are made of woodchips. Gallop tracks are longer and wider than the canter tracks.

If the trainer has the chance, the canter paths and gallops should be inspected after, as well as before, each day's exercise. Some stables have turf and/or sand gallops which need more care than modern 'all weather' gallops. Displaced turf has to be put back, or at least the holes filled with sand by the gallop man. It is also useful if the trainer can walk the gallops, especially if the following day is a gallop day. The trainer should look for the least churned up part of the gallops and send lot one horses up this part.

First Lot Work

First lot leaves the yard at around 7am for the canter tracks and gallops, usually walking part of the way. Road exercise is very good for strengthening horses' legs, especially yearlings and two year olds. A good work rider is required to lead the string out to the exercise grounds. If the horses go too fast they became strung out and, if the pace is not steady, the horses are always bumping and skidding into each other.

The walk to the exercise grounds helps warm up the horse and is considered by many trainers to be an important part of any training programme. Once on the exercise grounds the lot is broken up into groups of twos or threes or even fours.

The degree of work depends upon the nature of the exercise ground and, of course, on the fitness of each horse. Uphill canters and gallops put less stress on horses' front legs and are more effective in developing the muscles in the racehorse's back and hindquarters.

In the early 1950s, when Bill Marshall was training at Cleeve Lodge, Cheltenham, the only available gallops were up Cleeve Hill. He overheard two famous local trainers saying to each other that "Bill Marshall is training mountain goats this year". But it was a good year, proving the value of training on a slope, as he had 50 winners out of 20 horses.

An ideal gallop is up a hill that slopes at about a 35 degree angle making an ideal gallop and the gallop has to be at least four furlongs long. Four furlongs up the hill at three quarter speed is about equivalent to a mile at full speed on the level, while the concussive loading and stress level on the front legs is less than half. A trainer should never work a racehorse down hill as this work is extremely stressful for the horse's legs.

Gallop Days

On gallop days when first lot horses arrive at the exercise area they have first to be warmed up with a jog or a canter. For a fast gallop the grooms usually dismount and help mount up the more skilled jockeys and work riders. It is important that the work riders and jockeys keep the horse in balance and know at what pace the trainer requires the horses to run up the gallop. (The times and distances involved in training to win are dealt with more fully in chapter 10.)

The first lot is sorted into groups of two or three before they set off up the gallops. In any training exercise horses are encouraged to go 'on the bit' and horses within the groups should never be allowed to race one another. The horses are started off up the gallops at a steady pace and the riders gradually increase speed until they approach the last two furlongs or so of the gallop.

It is important that the horses in each group pull away together and it is undesirable if a horse pulls away late as its rider will have to let the horse off the bit to catch up with the rest of the group. This can be risky as pushing horses, especially young horses, at early stages of their training can do serious harm to muscles and ligaments. The speed and length of each gallop is set for each horse by the trainer before the gallop and during the course of the gallop, the work riders look at the trainer who may speed them up or slow them down depending on the horses' performance. Occasionally lot one horses are worked singly up the gallops.

It is important that the trainer waits at the head of the gallops to watch the work and to meet the riders as they come off the gallops. A very important part of training is the trainer's immediate assessment of the fitness of each horse as it is pulled up at the end of a gallop. This assessment will help decide future training requirements.

One important aspect of custom training horses is to identify how the state of the track or the 'going' affects performance. If a work rider always rides the same horse over the gallops he will get to know the horse's preference for the going. To run a horse which likes dry hard conditions on a race track where the ground is wet and heavy is courting failure. The assessment by a good work rider of a horses's capability and performance up the gallops is extremely valuable to a trainer.

Warm Down

A racehorse should never be pulled up suddenly at the end of the gallop (or at any other time) as this strains muscles, ligaments and tendons and makes the horse lame. After exercise it is very important that the horse warms down (see page 13, 95). Thus the work riders should steady canter for at least 100 yards after galloping before they bring the horses back down to a trot and then down to a walk for the return to the yard. In Britain the horses return to the yard at around 9am.

Second Lot Work

By around 10am the stable grooms would have washed down the first lot, given the horses a brush down and returned them to their stables, breakfasted themselves and started to brush and tack up the second lot.

The second string is broken up into groups of three or four horses by the trainer and again it is important to warm up (and warm down) properly. The second lot is the steady work lot and the horses are usually first trotted and then given two or maybe three canters. The groups of horses should canter at least four lengths away from each other and the groups are never allowed to overtake each other.

Third Lot Work

The third lot work follows second lot and contains the young two year olds. They are worked very easily for the first one to three months before being taken up a two furlong gallop for the first time. Part of the art of training is to decide the moment at which to gallop a two year old as this very much depends on individual horses. The racehorse's belly is a useful indicator - when the belly of a two year old 'tightens up' the horse is approaching the stage at which it can be galloped. They often start fighting for their heads and need some holding back on the bit. It is very exciting for the trainer when two year olds do their first gallop as this is the first time that the horse is really put on trial. But it must be remembered that horses improve all the time and the first gallop may be a disaster and yet the two year old could still become a world class sprinter.

Washing Down the Lots

After exercise and back at the yard all the lots would have had their legs washed down with buckets of warm water which are ready and waiting for the returning horses. It is important that the backs of horses' legs are well dried after being washed down and covering them with bandages is an effective way of ensuring that they dry out properly. If the wet mud is left on it is possible that the back of the pasterns, which have only a thin covering of skin, will become sore and develop horizontal cracks known as 'mud fever' or 'cracked heels'.

Riding Out

Some trainers ride out with the second lot. Bill Marshall did until he was 68 years old and he believes there are points for and against riding out. Points for are that the trainer gets the horses running at exactly the right pace as the work riders are forced to 'lay up' alongside the trainer; the trainer is with the riders which gives everyone a good sense of camaraderie; the trainer is amongst the horses and has a direct feel for their wind and gait; and the trainer can hear exactly what the riders are saying about their mounts. Against riding out is that it is impossible to assess the ability of the horses running behind, especially if the trainer's horse is going well, which can lead to horses being sometimes underrated. Overall Bill Marshall believes it is better for trainers to watch from the stable hack or standing. He rode out for years because he loved riding.

CHAPTER EIGHT   *The Art & Science of Racehorse Training*

Evening Stables

The afternoon routine is much the same in the tropics and in temperate climates except in the tropics, afternoon or evening stables commences an hour earlier at around 3.00pm. The grooms have a short afternoon break before they return to the yard. All the horses are led out and every evening, winter or summer, they should be walked rapidly for at least half an hour to stretch their legs and keep them from stiffening up. Then the horses are given a good grooming. In temperate climates such as in Britain most trainers use rugs to keep the horses warm in both summer and winter, unless it is extremely hot. In the tropics rugs are never used.

Head lad and trainer do the rounds of all the horses together. The trainer examines every horse: checking the grooming, the skin, the dock, the eyes, the nose, the back and all four legs. The head lad applies overnight bandages to any horse that is receiving treatment.

The horses are checked inside the stables under dim overhead lights - horses don't like bright lights - and this gives the trainer a chance to check that the removable mangers have been cleaned, the stable properly mucked out and that the bedding is in good condition. The legs of every horse in the racing stable are checked and the grooms asked, once again, if the horse ate up its overnight feed. One of the first key indicators of a problem with a horse in training is the horse going off its overnight feed and a careful trainer will continually ask the grooms about the way in which their racehorses 'eat up'. The trainer should ask how the horses 'came out' of their stables in the morning. Every trainer would like to hear that they came out 'bright eyed and bushy tailed'. After the horses have been checked they are fed. A thoughtful trainer will start at different ends of the yard each day, that way the stable grooms take it in turns to get away early.

Travel and Routine

After evening stables the trainer can return home, by then having worked almost non-stop for about 12 hours. On race days it is an even longer day. Bill Marshall recalls that when training at Newmarket it was not uncommon for him to travel up to Edinburgh and back down again in one day and it was sometimes hard to keep awake. He wrote off two E-type Jaguars, ending upside down in a ditch in one of them after falling asleep. The travelling became so bad that he started to fly to the meetings in a small private plane. Unfortunately on two occasions he had serious accidents.

"Once when flying up to a Scottish course with an owner, the propeller dropped off: I never knew where it landed. The owner went green but fortunately we had two engines - one more than the Spitfires I flew in the Second World War. We landed and arrived at the races on time. I was never sure if the large amount of whisky the owner drank that afternoon was to celebrate us arriving on time or to get over losing the propeller! One thing though he never flew with me to meetings again. I remember telephoning home that night to say I would be arriving late as we had lost a propeller - I was told to 'pull the other leg!'

"The other time was when I was flying to a classic race in Belgium. The plane crashed and the pilot was killed. My wife managed to pull me away from the wreck - even though seriously injured herself."

The Video
Despite live satellite television coverage of racing from many courses, most trainers still travel to the race track. Thus a trainer based in the south of England will have to leave the yard at 4am in the morning if racing in Scotland that day. Undoubtedly satellite TV has made life easier for the trainer, even becoming an important training tool. A trainer can now make a video of the races and replay it at leisure, studying what went wrong from the luxury of an armchair. It also means the trainer can spend less time travelling and more time training horses - and some time at home. Before satellite TV (and that other great help, an under trainer), trainers were often away six days a week, always returning home late at night and very tired.

Routine
Day in year out the routine continues. The successful flat racing trainer is hard at his job from the moment the young horses arrive at the beginning of the year to the end of the flat racing season which in Britain is

around the middle of November. If a trainer only trains flat racers then it might be possible to take a break in December. Traditionally British flat racing trainers spend Christmas in Barbados. But some train steeplechasers and horses for the flat with the result that their training season lasts all the year round since the British National Hunt season runs from the first week of August and continues to the first week of the following June. The jump trainers take a few weeks off in the summer if they are lucky.

Training horses can never be seen as just another job. The trainer is tied to the routine and the animals night and day. Physical stamina is required to deal with the long hours of the daily routine and emotional strength is required to deal with the excitement of the ups and downs of race days. The pressure is intense as the trainer has to have winners, for one whose horses do not win races is soon forsaken by the owners.

CHAPTER NINE

Training for the Jumps

The ditch.

The daily routine in a racing stables which specialises in training horses for jumping is basically the same as that described in the previous chapter on flat training. But there is one important difference - jumpers have to be schooled.

Flat Racers as Jumpers

The jump trainer is working with older, stronger horses than horses for flat racing so that if a horse is a disappointment as a flat racer at the age of four or five it might end up in a jump trainer's yard. It is an interesting phenomenon that flat racers that are not living up to a flat trainer's expectations may benefit from a short spell in a jump trainer's stable. Racing these horses over hurdles for a short season may suddenly improve their performance in the next season's flat races. The horse is usually a stayer and hurdling rekindles the horse's interest in flat racing.

The Jump Horses

Jump racing is a much more relaxed sport than flat racing. Probably because there is less money involved. There are no multi–million dollar yearlings with which to gamble, the stud fees are lower and there is generally less prize money. There is a greater sense of camaraderie among the jockeys and trainers partly because it is a dangerous sport - most jump jockeys break a lot more bones than flat racing jockeys before they finish their careers.

As a general rule jumpers are either mares or geldings. It is extremely rare that a stallion is a successful chaser although 'entires' can make successful hurdlers. When buying a jumper there is none of all the 'bred in the purple' hype that is attached to the yearling sales and a jumper's pedigree is less important than it is for flat racing. When buying a future jump horse the purchaser can either buy a three year old flat racer that he or she thinks will go well over the fences; a yearling or a two year old that has been bred as an 'out and out' steeplechaser; or a horse that has shown potential as a hunter and had success in point-to-point races.

Buying a Jumper

It is difficult to know if any yearling or even a two year old will be a good jumper - assessment of potential becomes easier after horses reach the age of three. Jumpers need to be strongly built (like sprinters on the flat) but of course they have to be stayers. If looking for a jumper in a flat racing stable, a strongly built, closely coupled stayer that has raced well as a three year old on the flat is often a good buy. A well balanced horse with an intelligent looking face, bright eyes and pointed ears is a good choice and an over-excited horse is always preferable to a soft-eyed, sulky one.

Bill Marshall believes that steeplechasers should first be raced over the fences when they are five or even six years old even though the earliest age British rules allow horses to steeplechase is four. Ideally he would start to train a potential chaser as a three year old, although the horse might not be raced until it is six years old, since the earlier the trainer starts the easier the horse learns. It is important to be extremely careful when first training young jumpers as bones are still not yet fully formed. In exceptional cases a jumper can race for some ten years.

Jumps and Fences

In Britain the important steeplechase races start in November with the Mackeson and Hennessy Gold Cups which are handicap steeplechases for five year olds and upwards. At every National Hunt meeting there have to be at least two steeplechases which are at least two and three miles long. Other steeplechase regulations cover the height, type and number of the fences per mile and although in the past there was a water jump and a ditch in each steeplechase, nowadays water jumps are optional. Sometimes because of their position the water jumps or ditches are considered too dangerous by the jockeys and they are removed from the course. For example the water jump at Ayr was taken out because the low winter sunlight reflected off the water straight into the eyes of horse and rider.

The water jump is at least twelve foot wide and guarded by a fence whose height is no greater than three feet. The ditch, six foot wide, is guarded by a board or a bank and rail which is no greater than two feet high. The ditch is situated on the take-off side of a fence which has to be at least four feet six inches high. There must be at least twelve fences, four feet six inches high, in the first two miles of a steeplechase and six in each following mile. Steeplechase fences are around two feet wide and made of tightly packed birch wood set in strongly built wooden frames. The fences can last up to five years if they are properly built with part of the birch being replaced before each meeting. The tops of the fences are repaired and patted flat by an attendant each time they are jumped at a meeting.

The Hurdles

Hurdles are multi barred, three feet six inches high, and resemble sheep hurdles. They are angled up at sixty degrees from the ground so that the vertical height from the padded top bar is three feet two inches from the ground. Horses take off from the inclined surface side and both the top wooden bars of hurdles and fences are often painted with bright fluorescent paint to make them visible to horse and jockey. At National Hunt meetings at least half of the prize money goes to the steeplechases, the rest going to hurdle races.

The Lot System

In Britain during June and early July jump trainers put their older National Hunt horses out to grass and start to bring them back in training in late July. Many use the same system of training by lots described in the last chapter, gradually building up the levels of work. Jumpers are started out in lot three and work up to lot one as stamina and fitness improves. There should be regular fast work days for jumpers (Wednesdays and Saturdays) and if a horse needs a lot of work to bring it to fitness, 'to hand', it should be sent out in two lots in one day. Jumpers are older than flat racers so they can take a tougher training regime than young two year olds.

Like flat racers no two jumpers are ever the same. Some may need cantering every day with two good gallops a week while others need half or even a quarter this amount of work. With jumpers, as with horses for the flat, it is important to take time in building up their fitness after a lay off. Thus much walking and trotting is necessary to bring the horse into condition. As a rule jumpers require longer and more steady work than flat racers as they have to race over longer distances. This work develops the aerobic pathway-respiratory system and slow twitch skeletal muscle fibres (see Chapters 1 and 2).

Horses new to jumping have to be schooled. If things go well, there is no reason why a trainer cannot send away a horse to a hurdle race or even to a steeplechase after six weeks of training.

One of the most important aspects in the training routine for jumpers is never to bore a jumper. In all training it is important to keep the horses interested in the work and this especially applies to jumpers as they become easily bored with jumping the same training fences time and time again. Once fit they should only be schooled once a week, just to keep them in 'trim'.

Schooling a Jumper

The golden rule when schooling a jumper is never to 'over fence' the horse. Racehorses in training must never lose confidence and the heights of the training fences should only be increased in line with the horse's ability. When first starting to train a horse to jump, a 'loose school', where horses are trained over jumps without riders, is an excellent training facility. The earlier a horse starts to jump the better, as young horses obviously learn faster than older ones.

Building Confidence

Some young horses have absolutely no confidence in their natural ability to jump. With this type of horse the trainer should start off by walking it over a telegraph pole that is laid on the ground until the horse shows no fear. Once this is accomplished the novice jumper is ready to be schooled.

Loose Schooling

Telegraph poles make ideal jumps for a loose school. Three should be laid across the straights of an elongated U-shaped track at about 20 yard intervals and one in the bottom part of the U, away from the bend. Telegraph poles are used so that the horse is taught to lift up its heels. When the horse has no fear of walking over a single telegraph pole it should be sent round the U-shaped track with a second older horse.

If the novice jumper was sent around alone, it could develop some bad habits such as jumping to the left or right, running out, baulking and whipping its head round. That is why, when loose schooling, it is advisable to send an older, steady horse who loves to jump with the novice jumper. The older jumper travels straight over the poles, sets a steady pace and the novice keeps up and learns to jump well. The trainer looks for the young horse to jump off on its hocks and glide over the pole at a shallow angle.

Loose schooling is an important part of training as it encourages the novice jumper to develop a fluid jumping style and the horse learns how to place itself when approaching a jump. Without loose schooling the novice horse jumps awkwardly which can make jumping difficult for the schooling rider and the gradual build up of confidence between horse and rider can become strained, perhaps irreparably, at an early stage.

The Schooling Rider

When a horse jumps well over the poles it is time for it to be trotted by the schooling rider over an adjustable bar. The wings or sides of the fence should be at least six feet high and made of solid wood and the fence wide so as to discourage running-out.

The bar should be solid but easily dislodged if knocked by the horse and the lowest position of the bar should be about 18 inches off the ground. At first the mounted, experienced jumper leads the mounted novice over the adjustable fence. Then the novice is taken over by the schooling rider who takes care not to ride too fast at the adjustable fence. The rider should approach the fence at a steady trot or a hack canter accelerating the mount into the obstacle and making sure that it takes off from its hocks. A good schooling rider, like a work rider for the flat, is invaluable to the trainer when preparing horses to race over hurdles or fences.

The Hurdle Stage

When the novice jumper can clear two feet six inches on the adjustable fence with confidence and style it is time to take the horse over hurdles, regardless of whether the young horse is to be a hurdler or a steeplechaser. The 'flights' of hurdles are specially prepared. The three foot six hurdles are packed with birch or gorse and staked into the ground but, instead of setting them up as they are on the racetrack at an angle of 60 degrees to the ground, they are set at a much shallower angle so that their vertical height is only about two feet six inches. This is the last height the novice jumper successfully cleared on the adjustable fence.

The mounted novice horse follows the experienced mounted jumper over the hurdles, then they jump the hurdles together and finally the young horse is ridden over the hurdles alone.

The Art & Science of Racehorse Training   CHAPTER NINE

Hitting the ditch: Concussive loading is enormous.

It is at this stage that the trainer begins to have a feel of the ability of the novice horse. Those horses 'with bags of heart' go at the hurdles, jumping them with relish. Unwilling horses have to be driven at the hurdles by the schooling rider and if necessary encouraged to go over with the whip.

The schooling rider should take off about half a stride away from the inclined face of the hurdle. Once the horse glides easily and readily over the flight, the angle with the ground is gradually increased until the hurdle's full vertical height of three feet two inches is reached.

Clipping Hurdles

Horses that clip the tops of the hurdles with their hind legs should not necessarily be discouraged since, providing it is a light blow and does not upset the horse's equilibrium, the racehorse is taking the shortest and quickest route over the hurdle.

The Steeplechaser

If the horse is strong, brave, performing well over the hurdles and looks as if it could easily clear a four foot fence, the trainer should try it on larger fences with the aim of making a steeplechaser. Trainers should always aim to turn hurdlers into steeplechasers as there is more prize money to be won in steeplechasing!

Training a Steeplechaser

If a horse coming in for training as a steeplechaser has not previously been hurdled (for example a horse that has been bred as a steeplechaser, or one that has shown promise as a hunter or done well at point-to-point races) it is advisable to first school it over the three flights of low hurdles (see above). Once proficient with the hurdles, the novice steeplechaser is loose schooled but this time setting up the U-shaped track with the telegraph poles raised some three feet off the ground. Once again a lead horse, this time a good and steady steeplechaser, is used to encourage the horse in training to jump the poles correctly. There are no sloping faces to the poles in the loose school so the horse has to gauge his take off well.

Adjustable Fence

If the potential chaser performs well in the loose school it is moved on to the adjustable fence. The bar is set at three feet and the height is increased in stages to about four feet. Once again the horse should never be over fenced and the fence height should be built up slowly and in parallel with the horse's confidence. Initially the schooling rider on the novice steeplechaser follows the mounted lead horse into the adjustable fence until the novice horse clears it well. Then the novice jumps the fence alongside the lead horse (on both its left and right sides) and then finally alone. The schooling rider concentrates on accelerating the novice into the jump, taking off correctly from the hocks and at the correct distance away from the fence.

Sometimes horses are jumped over flights of vertical hurdles topped with gorse which, at three feet six inches high, act as good preliminary obstacles before they go on to the tougher training fences.

Training Fences

Once the novice chaser is confident with the adjustable open fence and, if needed the gorse-topped, vertical hurdles, it is ready to tackle the tougher training fences. The training fences should be almost vertical, strongly built, faced with gorse or birch and about three feet six inches high. They should be slightly smaller than the ones the chaser would meet when racing. Once again the novice is run alongside a lead horse and then, later, on its own. It learns to respect the prickly, gorse-faced training fences, to take off early (but not too early) and to avoid catching the top of the fence with its hind legs - steeplechase fences are a lot tougher than the padded bar on the top of hurdles. Two plain fences and an open ditch is all that is required to train the steeplechasers. The horses meet their first water jump on the racecourse!

When schooling a horse to jump it is possible to train the horse every day over the hurdles or in a field with the practice jumps. It is practice that makes perfect and if things go well, it is not uncommon to send a horse away to race after six weeks of training.

Rest Days

On Sundays the horses in jump (and flat) training yards are rested. But the horses have still to be fed, watered and, around mid morning, led out of their stables to be walked in the yard. Then it is Monday morning. The daily routine for horses, trainer and staff starts all over again. Whether training for the flat or for the jumps the trainer has always one basic aim - and that is to win.

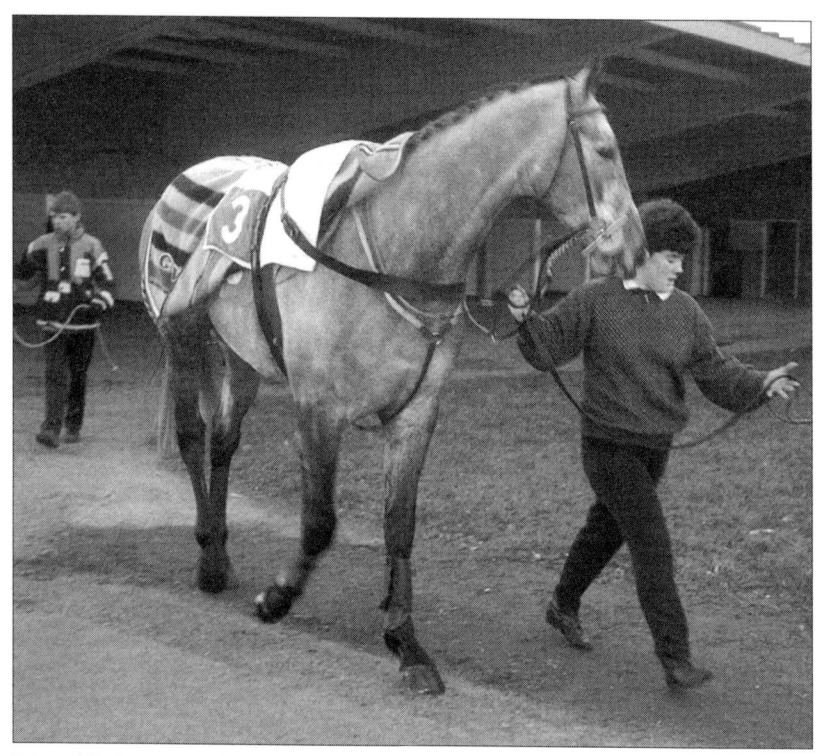

CHAPTER NINE *The Art & Science of Racehorse Training*

The saddled up jumper.

CHAPTER TEN

Training to Win

The undisputed winner.

Chapters eight and nine looked at the daily routines in flat and jump racing stables. This chapter looks in detail at the art and science of training to win: assessing the potential of the young two year olds, sorting them into sprinters and stayers and bringing flat and jump racehorses to their performance peak just before raceday.

Perhaps one of the first difficult decisions a trainer has to make when training a young two year old colt is whether or not to castrate (geld) him.

To Cut or not to Cut

Nowadays the aim of most British owners and trainers is to win a Classic race and then send the horse to stud to make a fortune in stud fees. If a young colt is well-bred, Bill Marshall believes in leaving the horse ungelded. Otherwise, for any moderate bred horse, castrate or 'cut' as soon as possible since as a rule geldings race better than colts. A colt is often distracted by fillies and if the colt is 'well endowed' it can physically be prevented from running at its best. The shock of the hind legs hitting the ground at full gallop can also be painful.

There is less of a problem with fillies and one advantage of purchasing a well bred filly is that if the horse performs badly on the racetrack there is always a chance that she could breed a winner.

The Cutting

Male horses are castrated by having their testicles and the associated ducts removed. Without castration, colts over two years old can become very aggressive and difficult to handle and have to be kept away from mares and fillies during the breeding season.

The castration can be performed under local or general anaesthetic and is usually 100% successful. 'Rough cut' or 'false rig' horses are geldings that show coltish behaviour and it is often thought that the testicles have not been completely removed at the time of the operation. This is unlikely however, and probable that the horse is just 'remembering' learned social patterns of behaviour. The coltish behaviour of a 'rough cut' gelding nearly always disappears with age.

A 'true rig' (cryptorchid) has one undescended testis and, because this undescended testis produces male hormones, even if the descended testis is removed the horse will behave like a stallion. The undescended testis can be readily removed by abdominal surgery.

Once the yearling is broken in and a decision made about cutting and it be can manoeuvred with the riding aids, the training programme is set in progress.

Flat Racing

As was seen in Chapter 8 young horses for the flat are trained using the lot system where they are gradually brought into condition by a steady programme of custom training. It is essential that the horse's progress through the lots is gradual and great care especially being taken not to overwork young two year olds.

Biomechanical Limits

It is thus important to train within the racehorse's biomechanical limits. In immature horses, bone has to be laid down slowly to improve strength and avoid deformation. Tendons and ligaments have also to be given time to grow and strengthen, and muscles must not be subject to excessive strain too early or else they may end up damaged. But some controlled stress helps strengthen bone and, as we have already seen, controlled training strengthens muscles and improves anaerobic and aerobic performance.

Overwork

It is important that work riders never work a young horse (or any horse) to the point of tiredness. A good rider can always feel when a horse is becoming tired and at this point it is especially dangerous to 'kick on' a young two year old. A tired horse becomes unbalanced and then tendons, ligaments and muscles can pull and tear as the horse makes bad movements.

Psychology of Training

Racehorses are naturally competitive but they may lose their will to compete. Thus it is very important to keep the young racehorse, and this also applies to any racehorse, in such a 'frame of mind' that it wants to race. This means training racehorses in groups when trotting, cantering and galloping, and never letting one horse outpace another in the group. It is the work rider's responsibility never to let his/her mount move ahead or drop behind another horse. From the onset of training a young horse should be exercised with others of the same age and advancement. It is part of the great art of training to avoid creating either an inferiority or superiority complex in a racehorse.

The final run: stride length may make all the difference.

Stride Length

Often races are won or lost by a few feet. With everything else being equal a few inches more in its stride length means that one horse will gain over another. Most unbroken horses have a naturally long stride when running free in the wild or without a jockey. When first broken in a horse tends to shorten its stride and the trainer needs to teach the horse to stretch out its legs again by working it with other horses. If the young horse is always dropping back it should be exercised with a different, slower group within the lot.

Sore Shins

Sore shins are usually due to an inflammation of the periosteum, the membrane that surrounds the cannon bone. Inflammation usually occurs on the fore legs and as well as in stuffy horses are frequently seen in two year olds who have just started training. Sore shins cause a shortening of the stride length and the cannon bones become painful to the touch when the trainer feels the front of the horse's legs.

The only cure for sore shins is rest - as it is in so many conditions which produce lameness in horses. As the condition improves the young two year old is eased back into lot three and training recommenced with light exercise such as walking on soft ground.

A good way of preventing sore shins in suspect horses is by fast walking them on hard ground or a road. This exercise helps build hard, dense bone.

Thick Winded Horses

Sometimes a trainer might have to increase the work load of a horse, especially a 'thick-winded', 'stuffy' horse to 'clear its lungs'. These are the expressions often used by trainers to describe the different levels of unfitness in a racehorse. They are, indirectly, using respiration rate as an indicator of fitness and this is discussed in more detail below.

When improving the wind of a racehorse (ie making it fitter) it is still important for psychological reasons not to let the horse get beaten, only to make it 'blow' harder. Thus the trainer should put the horse in a group alongside faster, usually older horses, to get its work rate up.

A 'thick-winded' horse has to be exercised hard and these horses often don't last very long as racehorses as frequently their legs cannot take the extra strain of the increased work load. A particularly common fault in these types of horses is fore leg 'sore shins'.

Training Ailments in Young Horses

As the trainer starts to increase the work rate, so do the young horse's ailments increase - jarred joints, knocks, cracks, stone bruises, windgalls are all regularly seen in young horses (see Chapter 14). Racehorses must be regularly checked for lameness, ideally twice a day, and at the first sign of trouble they should be rested. The trainer has to be very careful with the young racehorses and they should be 100% sound both when training and racing. However, as the horse matures some levels of lameness are sometimes acceptable (see Chapter 14).

Canters and Gallops

When the two year old horse is looking fit and has done a significant amount of trotting and cantering in lot two it is ready for a 'try out'. Prior to this the young horse will have been cantered in different ways. The canter can be broken down into three different grades of exercise: a 'tippity tip' canter which is just off the trot; a 'slow canter' which is a little faster; and the fastest canter which is the 'swinging canter'. After a steady exercise regime of tippity tip and slow canters the horse should be tried on a long swinging canter. If the horse is not blowing too hard after the long swinging canter then it is ready to 'try out' at 'half speed' up the gallops. Half speed is the usual pace for fast work on the gallops and, traditionally, it is called 'half speed' although it is much faster than half the horse's maximum speed or 'flat out' gallop.

Fast Work

In a racing stable the term 'fast work' means galloping a racehorse at around three quarter speed, never 'flat out'. Flat out galloping at the horse's maximum speed is usually reserved for the race track although short, 'flat out' test gallops are used by trainers to assess the racing potential of a horse.

The distance a young horse can run flat out at the race track is controlled. In Britain two year olds are not allowed to race more than five furlongs before the Derby which takes place at the end of May or the beginning of June. They are only permitted to run more than six furlong races after August.

The Try Outs

It is a key moment when a trainer runs a young two year old, would-be 'star horse' at half speed up the gallops for the first time. The millions of dollars spent in the sale room to buy the star yearling may have all been for nothing.

Different trainers have different methods on the 'try outs'. Bill Marshall runs the horse for three furlongs (one furlong = c. 200 metres) 'on the bit' and hopes to clock 15 seconds a furlong on a non-inclined gallop. He likes to see the horse working evenly 'on the bit', which means that it is responding to the least movement of the rider's hands, that its hind legs are driving it rhythmically along and the horse's back is relaxed. If the young horse does less than 15 seconds a furlong then it could be a sprinter. If the horse struggles to make the time it could be a stayer.

It is important to ensure that a slower horse is not just having a bad day by repeating the try out. If a young horse consistently struggles to do the speed, it is placed in lot two and carries on steady trotting and cantering for two more weeks before being tried out again up the gallops at 'half speed'.

Sprinters and Stayers

A horse's breeding will give the trainer some idea as to whether it is a sprinter or stayer, but it does not necessarily follow that stayer or sprinter parents will respectively produce stayer or sprinter offspring. The exercise regime for the offspring of stayers and sprinters is the same until the try outs.

The Lots

The try outs sort the two year olds into different lots and groups within the lots. Out of every 20 two year olds that come into training each year a trainer with 40 horses in the stables would expect at least four horses to be able to do 15 seconds per furlong without struggling at the first try outs. However a two year old not clocking 15 seconds a furlong at this stage of its training can still win sprint races at a later date: some thoroughbreds are slower to develop speed than others.

First Lot Try Outs

The fastest two year olds of the try outs are put into first lot and worked with steady exercise of trotting and cantering over a mile for a further week and then given a three furlong 'fast gallop'. The horses would *almost* be given their head' and ridden off the bit but the trainer should give the work rider instructions to never let the horse run completely flat out. And, even though the horses are galloping fast, the work riders should keep the groups bunched together such that they finish 'up sides', that is together and alongside each other. A potential sprinter should clock 11 to 12 seconds a furlong over three furlongs of a non-inclined gallop. If a horse runs the three furlongs in 33 seconds it could become a very good sprinter.

Then the trainer should return these young first lot two year olds to steady work for a further week before trying the fastest of the first lot groups up the gallops again, but now over a distance of four furlongs. If a two year old can run four furlongs in 48 seconds or less then the horse will probably be a winner. To have good horses capable of these speeds in a flat racing stable is exciting for any trainer, but it is important not to rush the training as it is always necessary to build a young horse slowly up to racing fitness.

The Long Fast Gallop

Bill Marshall believes that when galloping fast over five furlongs, a racehorse does not have the time to develop a proper breathing rhythm. The horse needs to fast gallop at least seven furlongs for the trainer to properly assess its ability and 'wind', an important, almost instant indicator of fitness and ability.

Towards the end of the first year in training he will fast gallop the two year olds over eight furlongs. If a horse is sweating freely, its sides are not heaving, it is not bleeding from the nostrils and it covered the distance in one minute 35 seconds (11.9 seconds a furlong) or less, then it is an exceptional racehorse. If it covered the distance in one minute 39 seconds (12.4 seconds a furlong) it is still a good racehorse and even a time of one minute 40 seconds (12.5 seconds a furlong) is acceptable.

The only time to fast gallop horses in training over eight furlongs is in these long, fast try outs. A mile fast galloped could take at least two seconds off a racehorse's performance if it were to be raced within 10 days of the mile gallop. Once the distance capabilities of a horse are known, as a result of the try outs, the trainer should avoid fast working the horse up the gallops for more than six furlongs. This is because long sustained gallops place enormous stress on tendons and ligaments and this applies as much to a five furlong sprinter as to a two mile steeplechaser.

A three mile steeplechaser might be fast galloped for seven furlongs but trainers should be aware that they could be doing more harm than good. The best place to fast gallop a racehorse is on the racecourse and not on the gallops.

Aerobic and Anaerobic Training

Once the trainer has decided that a particular horse is a stayer or a sprinter then the training programme is customised accordingly: Bill Marshall, for example, will use his 'lot system' to custom train. As a rule stayers need more steady work (aerobic training) while sprinters need more fast work (anaerobic training). This is because moderate sustained work improves (along with many other factors, see Chapters 1 to 4) the efficiency of the Aerobic Pathway, an energy production pathway more important for the stayer. High intensity work improves, also along with other factors, the Anaerobic Pathway, an energy prod‑uction pathway more important for the sprinter.

Rest and Work
After any severe work racehorses have to be rested so, even if the trainer is keen 'to bring on' a horse, it is important to remember that lot one horses are only galloped twice a week, Wednesdays and Saturdays, and meantime it is back to steady work, trotting and cantering, until the next gallop day comes along. The aim as always is to slowly build strength and fitness into the racehorse.

Fitness

Almost each day the trainer has to judge the fitness of each horse in the racing stable in order to create a custom training programme. Fitness is usually best assessed for first lot horses on gallop days when the trainer stands at the head of the gallops and watches each horse as it works its way up the gallops and as it is pulled up.

Work Rider
Much can be learned from the work rider. While the horse is on the gallops it is important to see that it is moving properly and a good work rider can tell immediately if there is something amiss, especially if the horse's gait feels awkward or if it is 'galloping lazily'.

Respiration Rate and Fitness
The first thing a trainer should look at when the horse is pulled up at the end of the gallop is its 'wind' - how much the horse is 'blowing'. A racehorse normally breathes about 10 to 12 times a minute when at rest, but this increases well over tenfold to around 150 times a minute in severe work. Racehorse 'fitness' can be measured by the speed with which the respiration rate returns to about twice above resting. This 'twice' is an arbitrary rate but, essentially, the speed of return can be used as an indirect measure of, for example, the speed at which the lactic acid levels return to normal which is used by some exercise scientists to assess fitness.

CHAPTER TEN   *The Art & Science of Racehorse Training*

A bright-eyed, fit horse ready for work.

Fitness is a reflection of the efficiency of the anaerobic and aerobic respiratory pathways and the efficiency of the functioning of the racehorse's different, complex, biological systems that have been discussed in some detail in the earlier chapters. Respiration rate can be and is used to measure racehorse fitness - the faster the return to resting levels the fitter the horse. After some 10 minutes following a good gallop, a fit horse will have its respiration rate down to about 20 breaths a minute, but it is always difficult to make hard and fast rules.

If the horse is blowing too much, its flanks heaving more than they should for that amount of exercise, then it has been overworked and needs a regime of steady, lot two work. In training parlance it needs to 'clear its wind'. Knowing the relationship between the 'blowing' and the amount of work required to 'clear its wind' comes largely with experience, but obviously the more the horse blows, the greater the work required to reach race fitness.

Again comments from the work rider on the horse's 'wind' during the gallop are extremely useful. Any hint of roaring, double wind or struggling for breath indicates future trouble. The trainer should always examine the nostrils after work to see that there is no excessive discharge which could be a sign of respiratory infection and make sure that there is no bleeding from the lungs.

Heart Rate and Fitness

In principle heart rates can be used as a measure of the fitness of a racehorse - the lower the heart rate for a given work load the fitter the horse. However heart rates are notoriously difficult to measure. They vary from horse to horse and many factors, especially stress, loud noises, an overfull stomach, or even the act of measuring, can dramatically affect the measurement. Little information can be obtained from a one-off measurement of heart rate, but a series of measurements taken at different times and under the same conditions can give the racehorse trainer useful information. Recently developed non intrusive heart meters can be used to measure heart rate while a horse is galloping.

The resting heart rate should be measured when the horse is as calm as possible, pre-exercise and meals, and resting values of around 30 to 40 beats per minute should be obtained. During heavy exercise heart rates for sprinters should vary between 180 to 250 and in a fit racehorse they should return to around 120 within five minutes following severe exercise - the 'warm down' period being part of this return period. Fit racehorses tend not to have significantly lower maximal heart rates than unfit horses, but on the other hand great racehorses, like top human runners, often have very low resting heart rates.

More simply the heart rate can be measured by listening to the heart beat. After the gallop the saddle is removed and the ear placed just below and behind the withers where the heart sounds and the rate can be heard. The heart beat can also be measured by placing the palm of the hand behind the elbow of either fore limb where the trainer should feel a 'hard' pulse.

At rest there should be a crisp not a slurred heart sound perhaps best described as 'lub-dup' and a steady heart rate. After work the trainer should hear a much faster, but still clean, 'lup-dup'. Any irregularities in the beat and sounds are obvious concerns. Heart 'murmurs', due to unusual heart functioning such as faulty valve functioning, are quite common in racehorses but often they disappear when the horse is worked - they can be debilitating if they do not. Training improves the speed at which the heartbeat returns to normal rates.

The methods of assessment of a horse's fitness are the same for a flat racer or a jumper.

Jump Training

Jumpers can be trained alongside flat racers and with the same exercise regimes although the jump horses will be in the slower lots. Once a jumper is fit, it is just a question of maintaining fitness between races. Jumpers are older than flat racers and, as they are in training for years, they have a greater chance of becoming bored with the training routine. If this happens the jumper quickly loses its edge and 'comes off the boil'. Jumpers can be hunted if the occasion arises and even hacked in the park to keep them interested in training and keen to win.

The Weaker Horses

The training regime is much the same for star and weak racehorses, for the flat or the jumps. The art with non-star horses is to find the right level at which to race them to obtain a win. The golden rule is not to run horses in races above their level for, once again, a racehorse should never be disappointed whether on the training grounds or on the race track. If it runs and neither wins nor 'makes the running' the horse will lose heart and this applies equally to a top class sprinter as it does to a horse running in a selling race. 'Heart' is an important idea in racing. If a horse has heart it will run faster than a horse which is fitter and stronger but does not have the will to win and to disappoint a horse with heart is one of a trainer's greatest crimes!

One of the most difficult tasks facing a trainer is telling an owner that their expensive purchase has no heart or is not up to scratch as a racehorse. Some yearlings will never make racehorses, no matter how hard the trainer works them. But owners become very attached to their horses and never believe it when they are told they are wasting their money by continuing to pay training bills. If a two year old will not do the three furlongs 'on the bit' in 15 seconds at half speed after six to eight months of training, it is usually pointless carrying on with the training programme.

Boredom

Occasionally some horses that have shown potential as say two year old flat racers do not live up to the trainer's expectations as three or four year olds. If the racehorse is good and there is nothing physically wrong with it, this inexplicable loss of performance is usually due to the horse becoming bored with the training regime or suffering from confinement stress. Bill Marshall had some success with 'exposed' horses that unexpectedly went off the boil and, most of the time, all they needed was a change of scenery. He would give them a rest in a stud farm, or try some new groom, or send a flat horse off to a friendly jump trainer or a jumper off to a friendly flat trainer - anything to give the horse a new perspective on life.

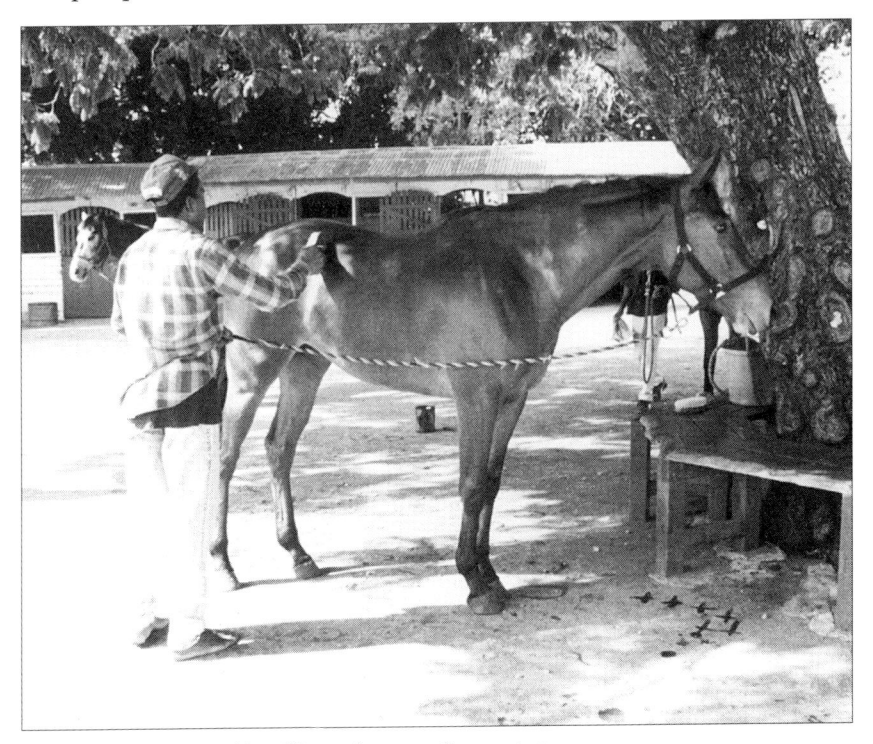

Frequent grooming and handling reduces confinement stress.

One of his most successful horses, a big grey called *My Swanee* was an exposed horse that he bought out of another yard. He sent him for three runs over the hurdles before flat racing and this stimulated its interest and, after training, *My Swanee* went on to win 22 races. The sprinter *Raffingora* was another exposed horse that, in two consecutive years, won eight races from 14 starts. *Raffingora* became the fastest racehorse ever over five furlongs from gates which it ran in 54.7 seconds at Epsom. That is just less than 11 seconds a furlong and Bill Marshall believes it is still a world record.

Race Day Approaches

For the fastest flat racers in their stables, trainers hope for a mild, wet spring and early summer so that, as race day approaches the horses can be worked hard up the gallops without risk of injury over hard dry ground.

Bringing a Horse On

The key and the art of training to win is in muscling up the horse through weeks or months of steady work and then keeping the horse at around three quarters of its maximum level of fitness. However, it is sometimes necessary to bring a horse up to full fitness quickly if, for example, the trainer and owner wish to enter it in a particular race at the start of the flat racing season.

Then, the horse is fast galloped three times a week instead of twice. Also the length of the gallop is progressively increased: first four, then five and then six furlongs. This should 'clear its wind' especially if the horse can be worked up a hill or a bank to avoid stressing its forelimbs too much.

Coming to 'The Boil'

Under normal conditions, when the trainer is not pressed for time, the racehorse is brought 'to the boil' ten days before the race so that by race day, and at the start, the horse is at its peak of fitness.

A first lot horse is kept healthy, interested and three quarters fit by trotting and cantering every day and on gallop days when it is worked at 'half speed' on the gallops at around 15 seconds a furlong for five furlongs.

Ten days before the race the intensity of the fast work on the gallops is increased. The horses are sent up the gallops with the trainer expecting 13 and then 12 seconds a furlong over the five furlongs. But always the pace up the gallops is set according to the fitness and temperament of the horse.

Jumpers 'boiled up' and ready to race.

The quickest indicator as to how the horse is responding to the increase in work is through its respiration. If it comes to the end of the gallop and is not blowing too hard the horse is approaching peak fitness and the work is decreased the next time out. This exercise regime required to bring a horse to the boil ten days before a race is the same for jumpers, stayers and sprinters although the trainer would, of course, expect slower times over the five furlongs for a stayer.

CHAPTER TEN — The Art & Science of Racehorse Training

The racehorse may be at its peak of condition but to win the race it has to be placed in the right race and that is probably the greatest art and science of racehorse training.

CHAPTER ELEVEN

Entering and Travelling

Loading can be difficult.

If the right horse is in the right place at the right time it will often, but not always, win. The 'right place' means that the trainer has entered a horse in the right race at the right course. This is easier said than done as every other trainer is trying to do the same thing. There are so many variables involved in horse racing it is surprising that 'favourites' do not fail more often.

The Entries

In all countries the 'Entries' are a skilled and complicated part of the art of training. They have to be made to the appropriate racing authority, stating which horse is running in which race and with which jockey. Depending on the country, some entries have to be made at least a week in advance of the race and a few days before the race the trainer has to declare that the horse is running. The trainer can then only pull the horse out of the race with a vet's certificate. The trainer can only change the jockey if there are valid reasons.

There are always more horses entered in a race than runners, and the longer a horse is left in as a possible runner ('stands its ground') the more it costs the owner to withdraw from the race. The aim is to know when to stand and when to pull, for it is useless to run a horse if there are two or three other horses in the race that are sure to beat it. A few days before the race trainers will talk to other trainers with regard to their runners in an attempt to sort out the situation to their own advantage.

Not only do trainers have to worry about the competition in each race, they have to choose the right race in which to enter a horse. The first problem is that there are many different types of races - races for horses that have never won a race (maiden races); races for either colts or fillies; races for specific ages; races for specific handicap ratings; races for specific ages and handicaps; weight for age races; sprint races; selling races where the winner is put up for sale; races for chasers and races for hurdlers; condition races which are not handicap races and so on.

The better the horse the easier the entry as there are less races and less classes although the entry fees and penalties for withdrawal are much higher. Throughout the world it is still every trainer's and owner's dream to own a star horse and win a British Classic race - the Derby, the Oaks, the St Leger, the 1,000 Guineas and 2,000 Guineas. However having a star horse in the trainer's stables produces a whole series of headaches, not least the worry of breaking down a multi million pound horse during training.

Handicap Races

The principal aim of the handicap race is that all the horses are meant to arrive at the finishing post together. A handicap rating is calculated on the horse's previous performance so as to give each horse an equal chance of winning a race and determining the amount of weight carried by the horse in its next race.

Abuses of the System

'Never bet on a handicap race' is the advice that is often given as it is the race most open to abuse and unscrupulous trainers see the Official Handicapper as someone to deceive. One well known abuse is when a trainer knowingly races a horse over the wrong distance. The horse fails to gain a place and its handicap rating is improved. Another is to race jumpers that have a tendency to jump one-sided, or lead to the left or right, on a 'wrong handed' course. Again the horse fails and next time out when it is correctly entered its handicap rating has been improved.

An unscrupulous trainer might enter two horses in a race, both of them with a chance of beating all the other runners. The trainer enters the two horses knowing that only the weaker horse will run and, at the last minute, the better horse is pulled out of the race but not before the trainer has obtained a good ante-post bet on the weaker horse.

Alternatively a trainer, working with a jockey, deliberately holds back a horse during a race when the jockey 'pulls on the bit' or deliberately places his horse behind a slower horse so as to improve its handicap rating next time out - and many more such schemes. The use of video play-backs of the race have helped reduce some of the abuses of the system.

The British 'Jockey Club'

For nearly 200 years the Jockey Club was the governing body of racing in Britain and responsible for stewarding races. It was formed in 1750, ten years after an Act of Parliament was passed that laid down the first basic rules of horse racing and officially recognised the sport. The Jockey Club was a self electing oligarchy and, although only initially concerned with racing at Newmarket, it controlled racing throughout the whole of the United Kingdom until 1993 when part of its role was replaced by the British Horseracing Board. The Board was created to look after the business aspect of racing as horse racing along with off-course betting is one of Britain's largest employers with over 100,000 people being employed in the industry. In 1992-1993, for example, the off-course betting turnover was £4.2 billion and in 1992 nearly five million people attended racecourse meetings. In 1993 despite the then deep economic recession in Britain there were 12,500 horses in training and 9,000 owners were seeking to share prize money that totalled £50 million. In 1994 Sunday racing and betting was finally legalised, which will increase attendance and betting turnover.

In Britain, Jockey Club stewards and their representatives continue to attend all meetings to ensure that the rules are adhered to and that 'integrity' of horse racing is maintained and that there is no doping of runners or any other illegal activities. The stewards are responsible for discipline and the Club's official handicappers decide the weights horses are to carry in handicap races. The Jockey Club's most famous handicapper was Admiral Rous (1795-1877) whose weight-for-age-scale still remains the basis of many famous handicap races. Rous's scale was in force until 1973 when it was revised by Jockey Club handicapper David Swannell. The government becomes involved in racing today through the Horserace Betting Levy Board where individuals are appointed by the government and the board is in charge of horse racing finance.

The Handicap System

In 1977 a handicap rating system was introduced, the official rating or International Classification, which nowadays is accepted for the best horses in Britain, Ireland, France, Germany and Italy. The speed with which the handicap ratings can be allotted or changed using computers, and the fact that horses cannot be pulled at the last minute unless they have a vet's certificate has, to a great extent, reduced the abuse of the handicap system.

Official Rating

Today the official rating expresses the form of a horse against the standard or 'norm' of 140 (10 stone or 140 lbs). Thus a horse rated at 140 gives 10 lbs to a horse rated at 130. The current rating system supersedes the 1973 official ratings when the norm was 100. The ideal situation for a trainer is to have a horse improving faster than its handicap rating and the worst situation is a horse that is constantly overrated by the handicapper.

Estimating a horse's handicap rating and doing the entries takes up a significant amount of a trainer's time. A British racing stable with 100 horses, having well over 50 race courses with some thousand races to choose from, needs to employ a full-time racing secretary whose job is to place the horses and study the race form. The form of every racehorse comes out twice a week during the season.

Handicap Assessment

Handicap races are much more difficult as there are so many different types of races and not the least of the problems is anticipating the official handicapper's rating for a horse and the distance. Bill Marshall has a rule of thumb which helps him predict what the handicap should be. If all things are equal - same age, sex etc - a win in a six furlong race means the horse will, next time out, concede two pounds for every length it won by. A win in a seven furlong race and the horse concedes one and a half pounds a length. A win over a one mile race and the horse gives away one and a quarter pounds for every length and a win in a one and half mile race and the horse concedes one pound for every length.

Group and Classic Races

It is easier for the trainer to place top horses in British Group and Classic races as the horses are raced on merit and not handicap. In the Derby all the colts carry 9 stone while the fillies have a 5 lbs sex allowance which is reduced to 3 lbs for the St Leger. In the 2,000 Guineas there is a 5 lbs sex allowance and in the 1,000 Guineas and Oaks the fillies race at 9 stone.

A yearling arriving in the trainer's yard in the autumn, purchased say from the Newmarket Highflyer sales and really bred out of the purple can be entered for any of the top flat races in Europe as soon as it arrives in the yard. In an extreme case if the owner buys an incredibly expensive foal out of some spectacular parents it can be entered in one or more of the top races as soon as the horse is born!

'Star' Horses

By the time the yearlings are broken in and have been exercised for three to four months and after the 'try outs' (see chapter 10) the trainer begins to have an idea as to how good the horses are - especially the multi million pound 'star' or 'big' horses. The pressure starts when the yearlings become two year olds in January and it is especially intense if the trainer has only one big flat horse in the racing stable. If the horse has the breeding and the potential to flat race as a three year old the trainer should avoid entering it in the most competitive two year old races during the first year of full time training. But there are no rules and that is why horse training is such an art. If the horse comes on quickly it may be that it will peak as a two year old and fail as a three year old.

'Star' British Horses

If a two year old can sustain around twelve seconds per furlong over four or five furlongs (see page 123) it is a potential star horse. As a three year old it might be a classic or even an Epsom Derby winner. If a British trainer's sights are on a classic race it is best if the star horse is not precocious, that is it does not 'come on' too fast.

To avoid the star horse from being 'knocked about' in two year old racing it should be entered for a maiden race around July or August. Then another race or two will build up experience before finishing the season. Then the flat racer is 'put away' for the winter and when it officially becomes a three year old in the following January the pressure is on to win the big race.

For the star sprinters in the stables and with perhaps the trainer's aim being the Epsom Derby, the first entry of the season might be the Craven Stakes or the Nell Gwyn Stakes at Newmarket or maybe the Classic Trial for colts and geldings at Sandown Park. The first classic race, the 1,000 Guineas for fillies, takes place in May at the Newmarket Spring Meeting. Then the first Wednesday in June is the crown of the British flat racing season, the Epsom Derby. After that the Irish Derby or the middle of June Ascot meeting for a race in the King Edward VII Stakes or, for fillies only, the Coronation or Ribblesdale Stakes. There is the St Leger in September and then in October the star horse could be taken to France for the Prix de l'Arc de Triomphe or, if the horse is invited, the Japan Cup in November.

The Cups

If the horse is a 'Cup-Horse', that is a top stayer, it could be entered for the Ascot Gold Cup, the Goodwood Cup or the Doncaster Cup. If the horse wins any of these sprinter or stayer races, it will be worth millions of pounds. At the end of the season, if it is a colt, it will be taken to the stud farm to continue to make its owner a fortune.

One of the many problems associated with entering a horse in a race is that everything may look fine on paper with the opposition, form, handicap rating, etc, but when the horsebox arrives at the track the horse has travelled badly and lost form.

Travelling

That the racehorse must arrive at the track in good physical shape is an important aspect of training to win. All the hard work employed in bringing the horse to peak condition can be spoiled by a mistake made during travelling – some horses can lose as much as seven to eight pounds in form, others lose significant amounts of body weight through sweating and anxiety.

Conversely a full day's travel and an overnight rest for a horse which is undisturbed by travelling can condition it as much as a gallop. In the box the horse is constantly working its leg muscles, relaxing and tensing them as the box sways along the road.

A good travelling head lad is important for a trainer as he quickly becomes aware of any horses which are travelling badly. Once a horse decides that it does not like to be moved from the yard it is often very difficult to make it change its mind – especially after the age of two. The trainer is then limited to entering the horse at racecourses that are within two hours drive of the stables. In extreme cases the trainer might have to walk the horse to the race track. Bill Marshall believes that some horses suffer from travel sickness but because of the nature of their anatomy they cannot vomit.

The Horsebox

Nowadays racehorses are more used to travelling. Most trainers have their own horseboxes and most horses can be trained to walk into them. Never frighten a horse with a horsebox and the best boxes are large, high, airy and well lit. Thoroughbreds first meet a horsebox as a foal, often travelling with their mother when she is to be covered by a stallion. Young thoroughbreds travel to the sale rings in horseboxes as yearlings and then on to the owner's or trainer's yard. There is some recent research that suggests that horses are less stressed when travelling backwards or sideways in a horsebox. Large horseboxes are now available where the horses are transported standing sideways or slanting across the box.

Loading

Some horses travel well once they are in the box but are difficult to load. When loading a racehorse into a box, its legs should be protected with boots or bandages. It sometimes helps to entice the horse into the box with a special feed and always helps to load the horse down–hill with the ramp facing up–hill. A very stubborn horse can sometimes be loaded by leading a rope behind its hind quarters and then pulling on the rope to move the horse forwards. In the last resort, a loud crack from the 'Long Tom' whip will usually shift the horse down on to the ramp and into the box.

Some horses are frightened by the sound of the clatter of their hooves on the ramp. The ideal solution is to have a gently sloping grassy bank leading up to a large brick platform. The horsebox backs up and lowers the ramp onto the brick platform. The horse is led up the grassy bank on to the brick platform and into the box across a level ramp. There is no clattering noise to frighten the horse as the ramp is supported along its whole length.

An effective method to train horses to travelling, especially consistently bad travellers, is to load and transport them to race courses at every opportunity. The bad traveller does not race, and is given a good feed at the racecourse, thus associating travelling with pleasure.

The racehorse's head should be held by a head collar attached by a slack rope to the box. It is important that the rope is slack and the horse is able to move its neck freely as this helps the horse keep its balance in the swaying horsebox.

Bill Marshall has had all manner of accidents in the tens of thousands of miles that he has travelled with his racehorses. Perhaps the worst was when he was sitting in the driver's cab when the driver had to brake suddenly for a car that shot in front of him. There was a terrible crash from behind and half a ton of horse suddenly appeared in the cab - it had shot through the partition bulkhead. There was a tangle of arms, legs and horse's hooves, men shouted, horns honked and the horse screamed with fear. Eventually it was dragged out of the cab and through the side door of the box. Incredibly, no one, including the horse, was injured. In Marshall's early days as a trainer it was not uncommon for horses to stick their legs through the floor of the box, and it was always the good horses that were the most accident prone!

Feed

If the trip to the racecourse is less than two hours the horse should not be fed. If the trip is longer and the horse not racing that day a hay net should be provided for the journey. Bill Marshall never gives hay on race days as he believes hay can stick in a racehorse's throat and affect respiration. He had experiences of this when he was in his early twenties and first started training in Australia and South Africa.

On long journeys of over 12 hours the horsebox should stop every six hours to water the horse and to try and make it urinate. Horses almost never urinate in the moving box as they do not like to splash themselves with their urine and they are unable to straddle. Once they arrive at the course and they are settled in the racetrack stables it is important that the horse urinates. If it doesn't it will not race well the next day. The grooms should shake up the straw beds and whistling seems to help. If a male horse is having difficulty urinating, he keeps drawing out his sheath.

After long journeys of 12 to 14 hours, the horse should ideally spend two or three days at the course before the race so that it can recover from the trip. Otherwise it is best if the horse travels to the track the day before the race and then returns home after the race or soon as possible.

CHAPTER ELEVEN
The Art & Science of Racehorse Training

Racehorses are creatures of habit and any short term changes in environment can upset them so the shorter the time spent away from the racing stables the better.

The Cargo Plane

Top quality racehorses are often flown overseas to compete. They are loaded by a lift into the hold of a cargo plane and during the flight they are kept in restrictive boxes. A small leather protective cap over the racehorse's head to protect its skull against the low roof of the cargo hold should be fitted. Usually the horses travel well in aeroplanes especially on short haul flights. In the Caribbean the local pilots are often more frightened of carrying the racehorses than the horses are of the aircraft! For very long haul flights horses are often given liquid drips to maintain their body fluids and given tranquilliser injections for the duration of the flight.

Occasionally a horse creates problems during loading into the aircraft and then may have to be given a tranquilliser. This means the horse would fail a drug test if raced within a couple of days of the trip, so this has to be considered when calculating the time spent away at overseas tracks.

CHAPTER TWELVE

Race Day

Gold Cup Day, Barbados.

Race Day is the terrible moment when the months or years of training either come to fruition or fail. There are so many factors involved in running a successful race that the trainer is busy right up to the start. His last act is to give final instructions to the jockey. Then it is up to the jockey, the horse and to some extent the hand of fate.

Before Departure

The first important job a trainer has to do on race day is to make sure that the right horse leaves the yard for the right race track! With three or four horseboxes running out of a racing stable each race day perhaps to different tracks this can be more problematical than it seems

CHAPTER TWELVE *The Art & Science of Racehorse Training*

- a travelling head lad is invaluable to the trainer during the loading up procedures. Before the horses leave the yard the trainer should also check that they are all properly shod or 'plated'.

Final Work Outs

If the horse is to travel and race on the same day it should be given a 'short', 'sharp' work out up the gallops on the day before the race. The sharp work out consists of two furlongs taken at half speed.

If the race course is over 200 miles away the horses will have travelled to the track a day or two before the race. Then the horse is worked in the early morning of race day - again two furlongs at half speed. Before galloping the horse should, of course, be warmed–up with half an hour of rapid walking followed by light trotting and cantering.

Feed

After the gallop the groom should rapid walk the horse to warm-down and then give the horse a thorough grooming before feeding. On race days all horses should receive half a bucket of water and their usual early morning mixture of nuts and oats but in much reduced quantities - a quarter to a half the normal feed. It is important that the horse is watered and fed on race day as a thirsty, hungry racehorse will not perform well.

On Arrival

On arrival at the track it is the trainer's responsibility to hand in the jockey's colours and to ensure that the horses have been properly declared for their respective races by the travelling lad. Runners usually have to be finally declared 45 minutes before the first race. The trainer should check the horses at the racecourse stables and then examine the state of the track. If possible the trainer should walk the course with the jockey (especially if it is a big race and there is time) to discuss its difficulties and quirks and pick out the best way round. Most good jockeys know each race course's peculiarities, such as the famous dip two furlongs before the winning post at Newmarket or the slope towards the rails at Epsom.

Saddling Up

Bill Marshall always saddles his horses and rarely has a saddle slip. The routine is always the same: bridle, breastplate, light latex pad for the saddle, weight cloth, number cloth, saddle, surcingle (a girth that goes over the saddle and is buckled up under the body) and finally when necessary the blinkers.

To prevent the saddle from slipping back he nearly always uses a breastplate which, when fitted, should be a small fist's distance away from the horse's chest. A second advantage of using a breastplate is that the girth does not have to be pulled too tight. He uses two and a half inch wide elastic girths and tightens them so that the horse can easily breathe. Some horses 'blow themselves out' when the girth is being fitted so a good jockey will always check the girth before the start of a race and, if necessary, get the starter to tighten it up a notch. As a rule, providing it is not too slack and thus dangerous for the jockey, the slacker the girth the better.

A trainer has to supply racing saddles for the apprentice jockeys but most of the top jockeys have their own - beautiful, ultra-light, flat racing saddles that weigh less than half a pound and have silk covered panels

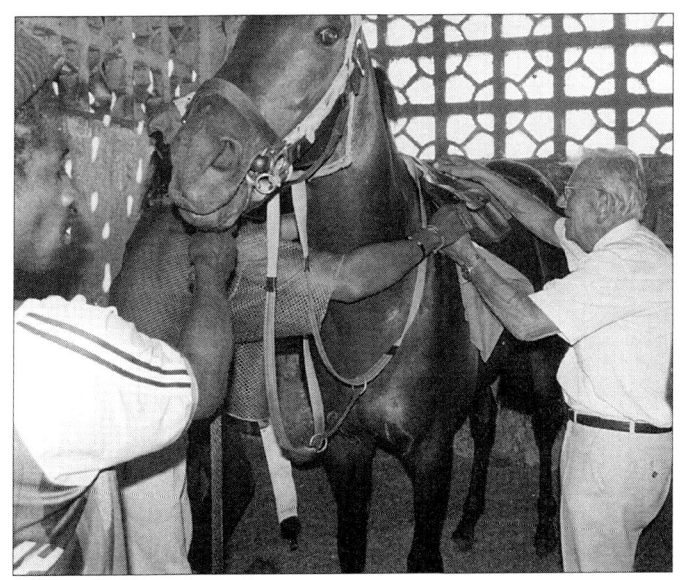

Saddling up.

and no stirrup bars. On these ultra light saddles the leathers are taken through a slot in the tree.

Bill Marshall never uses nosebands believing that they serve no useful purpose nor, for the same reason, does he use running or fixed martingales that are meant to lower the head of a horse and increase control. He does use an 'Irish martingale' or 'Irish rings' or 'spectacles' as they are variously known. An Irish martingale is not a true martingale, as it only affects the direction in which a rein is pulled, and consists of a six to nine inch leather strap with a ring at each end through which the reins are passed.

Bits

Fitting the racehorse bit correctly on race day is as important as fitting the saddle. Racehorses take a strong hold of the bit so the bit must sit comfortably at the back of the horse's mouth. Most racing bits are loose ringed jointed snaffles and they allow a fair amount of play of the bit in the horse's mouth. They act like nutcrackers on the sides of the jaw of the horse's mouth and the joint can hit the roof of the mouth painfully if the bit is pulled too sharply. The snaffle bit lies over the tongue and on the 'bars' (the gum that lies between the front and back teeth). If a horse has a tendency to pull very hard the trainer might use a snaffle made up of chain links, a twisted snaffle, or in extreme cases of pulling or boring when the horse keeps pushing its head down, a gag snaffle. 'Draw reins' that pass from the saddle through the rings of the bit and back to the jockey can be used as a further aid in controlling horses that pull hard.

A racehorse tends to produce a lot of saliva when the racing bit is fitted, partly due to the stimulus of the bit in the mouth and partly the excitement, which the horse picks up, of race day. To settle the horse and to increase its comfort the mouth should be sponged out with fresh water just before it is ready to leave the saddling up stable.

The trainer should use the lightest possible bit and bridle since carrying any extraneous weight slows up a racehorse. Even though the jockey does not weigh in with the bridle it is still an extra weight that has to be carried by the horse. Light racing snaffle bits are made of aluminium alloy, while loose ring mullen mouth snaffle bits, for horses with sensitive mouths, have a thick rubber bar.

Blinkers

The last piece of racing tack to fit is the silk blinkers. Some horses improve substantially wearing blinkers, others, especially fillies may 'sulk' in them. The trainer finds out during training if a horse needs blinkers. A horse will usually benefit from blinkers if it constantly turns its head round to look at the other horses in the group. It is usually the work rider who will be the first to notice this bad habit. Blinkers stop this type of horse from losing concentration. Another use of blinkers is when a horse is 'whip shy' - blinkers prevent the horse from noticing when the jockey reaches for his whip. Half blinkers are preferable to full blinkers.

The Jockey - Trainer Relationship

The relationships between horse and jockey, and jockey and trainer are incredibly important in winning races. A trainer and a jockey must have complete confidence in each other and this confidence is hard to create and difficult to keep. Competitive horse racing, by its very nature, gives trainer and jockey ample opportunities to become dissatisfied with one another. In a field of 12 horses usually five of them, through handicap, natural ability and level of fitness, have a real chance of winning. But there is only one winner so, for every race, there are at least four disappointed jockeys and at least 12 disappointed people if owners and trainers are included. The jockey-trainer relationship has a better chance of surviving nowadays because video recordings enable the race to be analysed and blame can be apportioned when and where necessary.

A Good Jockey

A good jockey always rides a racehorse with some light pressure on the bit. At full race gallop with the jockey standing in the stirrups, crouching behind the head to reduce wind resistance and with knees into the horse so that the lower leg can drive the horse to the finish, the good jockey avoids pulling on the horse's mouth in order to maintain balance. The racehorse must be allowed to extend its head when racing with the jockey placing a minimal amount of pressure on the bit. That is until the end of the race when some jockeys lose contact and allow the head to fully extend as the racehorse approaches the finishing post. A few extra inches can make all the difference in a photo-finish!

Horses are temperamental: some horses will run for any jockey, others will not; some have to be coaxed along or held back until the last few furlongs; some hate the jockey's whip while others need it; some horses prefer to lead from the front while others from behind; some are slow starters and others leap out of the stalls too fast; some are bullies, others cowards; some full of heart, others lazy and so on.

These psychological characteristics of a racehorse have to be observed by the trainer during training and this information passed on to the jockey, especially if it is the jockey's first ride on the horse. The horse's character and ability will, to a great extent, influence the 'orders' the trainer gives the jockey before the start of the race. A good jockey can ride any racehorse, riding the horse according to its temperament but the jockey can be much helped during the race by correct instructions from the trainer. Good jockey's ride races with a steady rhythm and, most important of all, in balance. They will keep their mounts running in straight lines and take them, when they can, round the inside of bends next to the rails.

The jockeys will all have done their homework: learnt all they could about their own rides as well as studying the form of the other horses and their jockeys. Today the brilliant jockeys are the 'kings of racing', earning fabulous money, but for every successful jockey there are dozens of good, average ones and jockeys that have failed through injury or other reasons. Horse racing, especially steeplechasing, is a dangerous sport, and the jockeys that become famous deserve the praise and the money.

Winning Races

Race tactics are also incredibly important in winning races and the trainer as well as the jockey has to know the form and characteristics of

The Art & Science of Racehorse Training   CHAPTER TWELVE

the other horses in the race and the form, ability and weakness of the other jockeys.

The trainer has to know how a jockey rides before deciding to give a particular horse to a jockey. Just as there are horses for courses there are jockeys for horses. In classic races and trials, for example, often a change of jockey will bring about a change of winners. A hard riding jockey, like Lester Piggot, drives the horse with hands, heels and whip. Others, like the now retired 'Scobie' Breasley, sit quietly on their mounts, riding the shortest route, picking the ground and getting the best out of the horse without flourishing the whip. Piggot and Breasley, two superb jockeys, demonstrate two different styles of riding, neither one necessarily better than the other, but their different styles of riding suiting different horses. Lester Piggot has a tremendous will to win and is particularly good with 'lazy' horses.

Saddled up.

The key features for winning any race are a balanced horse at the peak of its performance, intelligent riding and the use of pace. The brilliant jockeys are intelligent and have an instinctive feel for balance and pace. Clever jockeys set traps for the unwary and will try to squeeze jockeys across to other horses or to the rail as they start to make a run or a break, or they force other jockeys to pull up and unbalance their mounts. They watch out for mistakes by the other jockeys and for any traps they might set them. They will try and obtain information from the other jockeys before the start of the race about their tactics. But a

149

good jockey will never deliberately ride foul - for example, unbalancing a rival jockey by tipping him up with a foot under their stirrup, holding back, bumping or cutting across other horses.

Jump jockeys have to have all the same abilities as flat race jockeys, plus they have to know how to jump! Jump jockeys generally ride with longer stirrups and tend to bring their feet forward and keep their bodies at right angles to the ground as they approach the landing. As soon as the horse lands the jockey returns to the flat racing position and on the run in to the winning post they have to ride as well as any flat race jockey.

The Race

A good flat or jump jockey will ride the race at the right pace for their horse - this requires an instinctive knowledge of their mount's top speed. The jockey will, for most of the race, keep the horse racing at just below top speed, regardless if the horse is first or last. A jockey must have some extra speed to produce when needed and this may or may not be at the finish. Acceleration may be required, for example, to swing the horse to the outside of the leaders, or a sudden increase in pace may be needed to enable the jockey to keep contact with the leaders. If the jockey has the horse 'flat out' all the time it is extremely unlikely that the horse will win unless it is so fast that the opposition fades away completely. A horse running flat out over the distance will, as soon as it starts to tire, shorten its stride and that loses races.

Jockeys must not become 'boxed in' behind other horses, or stuck on the rails with no way out. They must never accelerate or decelerate too quickly as loss of rhythm and changes of pace are very tiring for all racehorses.

The Finish

Racehorses are trained to take a hold of and lean into the bit. Slacken the reins suddenly or by too much and a racehorse will trip forward. As the horse extends and pulls back its neck during the gallop the jockey has to move his or her hands back and forward as much as two feet so as to keep a steady but light pressure on the rein.

The moment when the jockey times the final run is critical. The horse has to be in the right tactical position with a clear sight of the post and a run in on a straight line. The horse should be in balance and the correct distance from the post to suit the temperament of the horse: run too soon and it runs out of energy, too late and it will be out of touch with the front runners.

Close to the finish, the most critical part of the race, the pressure on the horse's mouth should be gradually reduced by the jockey and the horse ridden off the bit, but ideally there should always be some slight contact with the mouth. The jockey's hands should go well forward to allow the horse to have a free head and neck and the jockey's legs go back to encourage the horse to stretch out its stride. After the racehorse's legs power drive it completely off the ground the jockey's legs and hands return. This rhythmic 'scrubbing', that is moving the hands forward and the legs backwards and then the legs forward and the hands back, must be carried out in rhythm with the horse's movements. Throughout the jockey grips the horse with his or her knees.

If racing to beat another horse at the finish the jockey attempts to scrub at a slightly increased rate, at the same time kicking the horse on and squeezing with knees and legs. The jockey must only increase the scrub rate in tune with the horse, never scrubbing faster than the horse can gallop. Good jockeys have an instinctive feel for rhythm and balance of an accelerating horse and are able to increase the horse's speed without losing rhythm. As the jockey approaches the post, if necessary, he forces an increase in pace with the whip.

The Whip

Nowadays there is much controversy about the use of the whip. Over use can turn good racehorses sulky and sour and they may never want to race again - especially two year olds. A lot of the time good jockeys do not use the whip, just 'breezing' it over the horse's backside but some racehorses respond well to the use of the whip. When the jockey uses a whip the quarters (not the flank or stifle) have to be hit on the correct side: usually the left side as most horses have a natural tendency to move to the left.

The Aftermath

When a horse wins a race it is a great triumph for the jockey and owner and a tribute to the art and science of the horse's trainer. Then, after the euphoria of the winner's enclosure, the owner celebrates with champagne, the jockey considers the next ride and the trainer saddles up the next runner before giving final instructions and returning to the owners and trainers enclosure for the next race.

Bill Marshall: "If you get all the many details of training and tactics right, and if you are lucky on race day, you will have winners. But despite all the trainer's efforts some races are just won on luck and, believe it or not, I am superstitious. I never turn back once I've left the house for the track on race days; I never have any green in my own racing colours which are pink and blue; and I believe we shouldn't take photographs of the horse until the finish!

Often, at the end of race day after the horses had run and I had talked over the day's meeting with the owners, and discussed future plans, finally I would head for home. When I arrived, there would usually be a message from the head lad asking me to check some of the horses before work in the morning. So out I would go again. I would have just returned, settled down in my arm chair with a sigh and a large scotch, when the telephone would start to ring: 'What happened today Bill?' or 'Bill I see you have got some runners at Doncaster tomorrow, do you fancy any of them?' ... I start to think of bed for I will have to be up at 5am the next day."

Racehorse training is indeed a dedicated profession.

CHAPTER THIRTEEN

Conformation and Condition

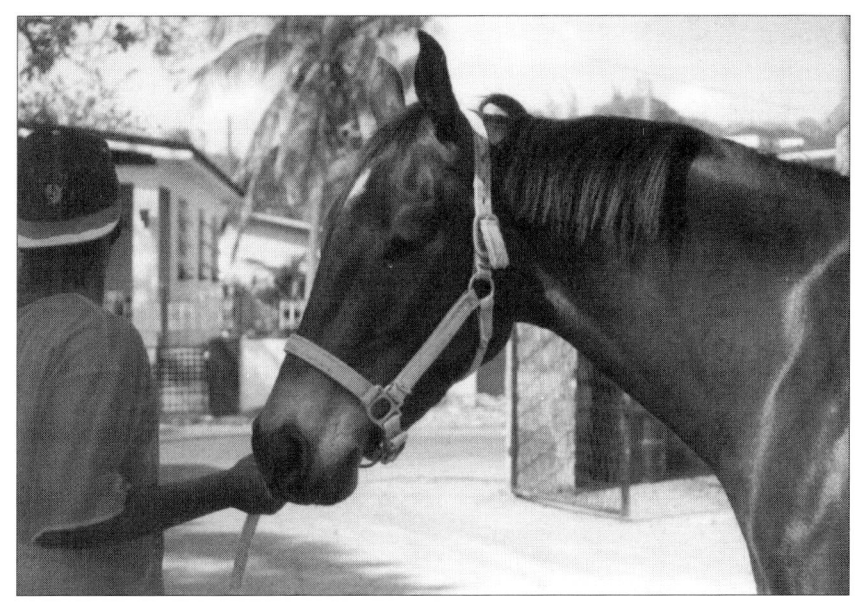

A beauty or a beast?

Horse racing has its own peculiar magic and the 'pleasures of the turf' captivate millions of racecourse goers and armchair participants each year. But few people, except perhaps bookmakers, make a lot of money from racehorses; it is especially true of owners. Unless owners treat owning as a big business and invest millions, their racing is unlikely to become profitable. Top horses can make millions of dollars in prize money - but there are only a few big races each year and only one horse wins each race.

Until very recently Britain's owners had about a ten per cent chance of breaking even. In 1991 a report on horse racing commissioned by Lord Zetland found that British owners were spending £220 million for £22 million of prize money. However prize money in Britain, for example, is increasing as are racecourse attendances. In the United States there is about a fifty percent chance of breaking even; and slightly more in the Caribbean.

Owning winners of classic races is probably the most lucrative aspect of horse racing. These horses, especially if they have a good racing pedigree, are worth and sold for millions of pounds. If the horse is a stallion then he will make his owner another fortune away from the racecourse at the stud farm.

Another less glamorous way of making horse racing pay is to buy horses that are undervalued because they look like losers but are in fact winners.

Conformation and Soundness

A racehorse's performance is generally considered to be due to conformation and condition. Conformation is genetically determined and so changes only with growth and age. A truly 'sound horse' is one which is as healthy, or in as good condition, as its conformation allows. If poor conformation affects a racehorse's performance nothing can be done. However, if the racehorse is unsound and providing the unsoundness is not due to an hereditary disease, modern veterinary medicine and custom training can reverse this.

Most racing people have a clear idea about conformation. Bad conformation will often lead to unsoundness, but not always, and the skill and art of buying a racehorse cheaply is to recognise those aspects of bad conformation which do not compromise a racehorse's performance. Badly conformed horses always sell for less money and this is where the owner/trainer can make spectacular gains. Some trainers, including Bill Marshall, have had some great successes with buying cheap racehorses that were in bad condition and, conventionally at least, badly conformed. These horses go on to win lucrative, top class races.

Good Conformation

Any racehorse regardless of age should have a bouncy, easy action with its legs working parallel; a good length from shoulder to buttocks, a strong neck and a deep girth and loins; a strong back, high withers, wide gaskins and straight hocks and everything in balance. The musculature must be symmetrical with no wastage (atrophy) on either side when the horse is viewed from the front or the back.

The foreleg knee and fetlock joints should be large, solidly constructed and free from any swelling. A knee that is set backwards is prone to small fractures of the carpal bones almost as soon as the horse starts to work. If the pasterns are too upright they will not disseminate foreleg concussive loads; too long pasterns and the leg doesn't drive the horse forward properly. The hind legs should have large, solid hocks and fetlock joints which again should not be swollen. The hock should be straight for a powerful drive. As a general rule sprinters are more powerfully built than stayers.

Feet are an important part of a horse's conformation and they are often overlooked. Feet should be the same size with strong frogs, deep heels and even wear. When the horse is in motion the feet should rise equally on either side.

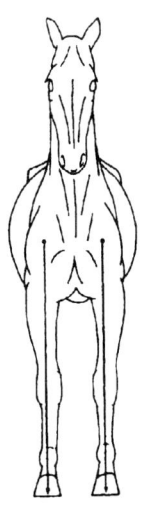

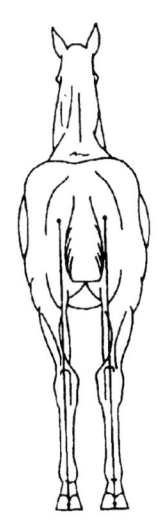

Figure 13a & Figure 13b: Good Conformation (after P.C. Goody).

CHAPTER THIRTEEN *The Art & Science of Racehorse Training*

The ideal forelimb has a wide, strong sloping shoulder and if an imaginary vertical line is dropped down through the knee, cannon and hoof (Figure 13a), this line should divide the limb in two. The best conformation of the hind limb is a thick well rounded thigh and when an imaginary vertical line is dropped down from the point of the buttock through the middle of the hock, fetlock and hoof (Figure 13b), it should divide these regions in two. The imaginary lines up each forelimb and hind limb should run parallel.

Bad Conformation

Too heavy a head unbalances the horse, but badly made mouths are not necessarily a problem. However narrow nostrils, jaw and throttle all cause respiratory problems and roarers and whistlers should always be avoided. Since there is evidence that these conditions are inherited an afflicted horse should never be sent to stud.

'Out-bowed' or 'crooked-legged' forelimbs are unacceptable in any racehorse. The hooves are in the correct position, relative to the normal parallel axis, but the limb is bent outwards in a bow (Figure 13c). Out-bowed forelimbs throw stress on the knee ligaments and the fetlock

Out-bowed
Fig 13c

Closed in front
Fig 13e

Cow-hocked
Fig 13d

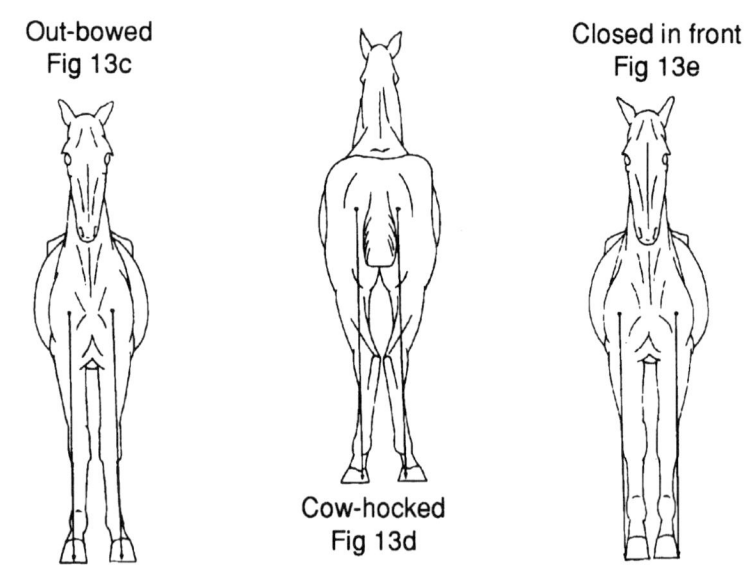

Figures 13c, 13d & 13e: Bad Conformation (after P.C. Goody).

The Art & Science of Racehorse Training CHAPTER THIRTEEN

and neither will stand up to the stress of racing. A 'cow-hocked' horse, where the hocks are bowed inwards (Figure 13d), puts undue strain on the hock and often leads to bone spavin (see next chapter). Out-bowed forelimbs and cow-hocked hind limbs are sometimes found in the same horse.

A horse 'closed in front' will not make a racehorse (Figure 13e) as the fetlocks and ligaments of the knee will not stand up to exercise. The front feet are too close together and this often occurs with a weak, narrow, unmuscled chest and a horse which has 'poor wind'. Closed in front often occurs with hind limbs being 'closed behind' (Figure 13f).

Acceptable Conformations

'Closed behind' is a less serious condition than 'closed in front' and, providing the racehorse is not also closed in front, a small degree of closed-behindness (Figure 13f) is tolerable.

Another acceptable conformation is when the thoroughbred is said to be too 'open in front' (Figure 13g). This may be associated with strong, even excessive, muscle development of the body which can also result in the horse being too open behind (Figure 13h). A well muscled

Closed behind
Fig 13f

Open in front
Fig 13g

Open behind
Fig 13h

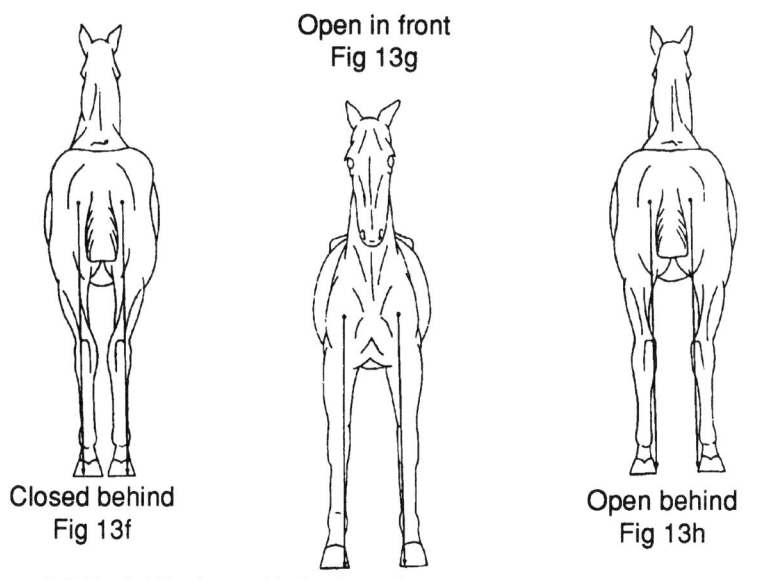

Figures 13f, 13g & 13h: Acceptable Conformation (after P.C. Goody).

thoroughbred that is both 'too open in the front and behind' can be a very good racehorse. A horse in bad condition can also be 'too open in front' but this can be corrected with the right diet and exercise.

A racehorse can be 'cross footed in front' or 'pigeon-toed' providing the condition is not too extreme (Figure 13i). The hooves hit the ground irregularly and wear unevenly, stressing the inner bones of the foreleg but, if the horse is strongly built, this will not affect performance. *Raffingora*, a big grey sprinter Marshall once trained and who became the fastest horse in the world over five furlongs, was cross footed in front.

When the knee is pushed inward as in a 'knock-kneed' or 'ox-kneed' thoroughbred (Figure 13j) or when the hind limbs are 'bowed' (Figure 13k), providing these features are not too severe the racehorse's performance may not be affected.

Trainers and owners can often obtain very good bargains when purchasing acceptably conformed thoroughbreds (Figure 13f – 13k) that are in poor condition. The physical state of the racehorse, that is its condition, is generally dependent on external factors. If a racehorse is in bad condition, its performance can usually be improved through proper diet and custom exercise.

Cross-footed
Fig 13i

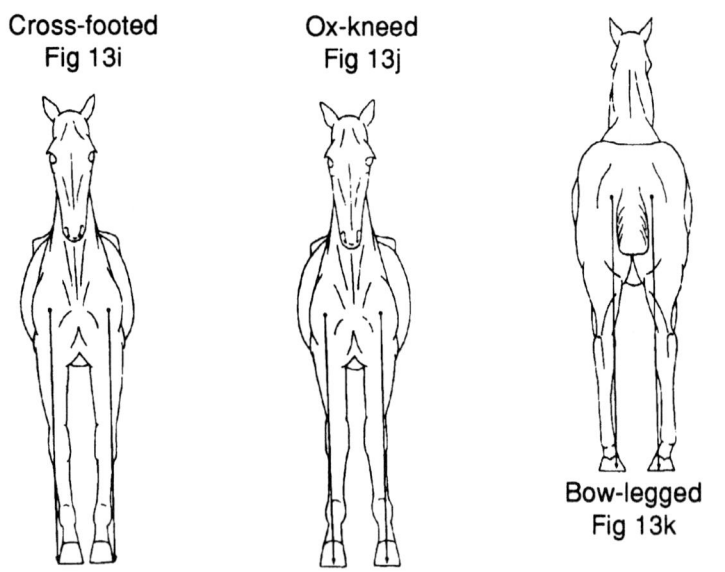

Ox-kneed
Fig 13j

Bow-legged
Fig 13k

Figures 13i, 13j & 13k: Acceptable Conformation (after P.C. Goody).

Condition

Racehorses need to be examined daily for any loss of condition.

Loss of Condition

Often the first sign of trouble is the horse not eating properly. Hence during the daily routine examinations the trainer should ask the horse's groom 'did it eat up?' Racehorses that are especially highly–strung racehorses will for no apparent reason suddenly go off their feed. This often happens just before or after a race with the result that there is a serious loss of condition. The trainer should continue to exercise the horse, but only steady work, trotting and perhaps a light canter. The horse should be tempted by adding honey or molasses to its feed. If that doesn't work a course of iron and B_{12} injections will often relieve stress and bring the horse back on its feed. The injections have to be stopped three days before a British race because of rules relating to drug abuse. If the horse continues to refuse its food the trainer might suspect a sub-clinical viral infection and the vet should be called and the horse's blood tested.

Mouth and Teeth

The racehorse's mouth is an important part of its general fitness and regular examinations help to keep the horse in good condition. The horse might be off its feed because of the state of its teeth. If its breath smells this is often an indication that there is a mouth infection or teeth problems.

The difficult period for teeth is when the racehorse is between two and four years old, when the temporary teeth are being replaced. (There are usually less problems when the third set of incisors are replaced at five years.) When the first set (middle) incisors are replaced the palate just behind the teeth can become swollen and sore. Unfortunately this coincides with the period when the horse is undergoing intensive flat race training and a young racehorse will reject the bit if its mouth becomes uncomfortable because of teeth problems. The first teeth are soft and can become jagged. They may need to be filed down and troublesome 'caps' which lie over the pre-molar teeth may need to be removed. A horse's incisors and molars grow throughout its life, but normally the rate of tooth production is equal to the rate of wear. If there is a small misalignment of the jaw, the teeth do not grind down properly and they have to be rasped back.

Body Temperature

A small rise in the core body temperature is an early indication of potential problems with the general health or condition of a racehorse. The core temperature is taken by passing a vaseline coated thermometer two or three inches into the anus of a horse for a couple of minutes. A useful trick is to hold up the horse's tail with one hand as (unlike mules!) a horse with its tail in the air does not kick. Normal body temperature varies from 38 to 38.2 degrees Centigrade (100.4 to 100.8 degrees Fahrenheit). Core body temperature stays surprisingly stable even after exercise so a rise of one degree Centigrade is cause for concern. As soon as a horse starts to run a temperature it should stop all work. Usually the vet will place the horse on a course of general antibiotics, but it is important to find the reason for the rise in body temperature.

Ticks

Ticks can rapidly reduce the condition of a racehorse. Ticks feed by sucking blood and there are a number of different species of tick. In the tropics ticks can spread biliary fever (*babesiosis*) which appears as a loss of appetite and fever and the urine can become brown with destroyed red blood cells. Some species of tick can cause paralysis if there is a very heavy infection. The female tick injects a poison into the horse as it sucks the blood which, if the tick infestation is great, can eventually stop the heart. Removing the ticks at grooming will help prevent biliary fever and tick paralysis. A horse with *babesiosis* may take months to recover following a course of drug treatment.

Worming

Most horses are infected with some species of worm. Racehorses with worm infections rapidly lose condition but regular monthly worming medicine will keep both white and red worm numbers down and reduce the risk of cross infection in the racing stable.

Most worms spend some part of their life cycle in the horse's gut where they reproduce by laying huge quantities of eggs which pass out with the droppings. The larvae then infect other horses.

Red Worms
'Red worms' (strongyles) are red because they often suck the horse's blood and in extreme infestations can cause fatalities by physically blocking a horse's blood circulation. They can be up to two inches long and there are dozens of species. *Strongylus vulgaris* larvae attack the small blood vessels in the gut and as a result the horse may suffer from spasmodic colic.

White Worms
'White Worms' (*parascaris equorum*) can be up to a foot long and in extreme infestations can multiply to such an extent that in young horses they can block the gut.

Colic
One of the most common complaints racehorses suffer from is colic or abdominal pain. Colic is always a worry for a trainer, its causes are numerous and its effect can range from the mild to the fatal. Racehorses are confined and fed artificially, which must induce some stress in to the racehorse's life, and confinement may even induce a sort of 'digestive stress' resulting in colic. All signs of colic should be treated seriously: the racehorse should be put into a loose box with water and no food and the vet called. A racehorse with colic is clearly in pain and moves about restlessly pawing the stable floor and looking round at its flanks. The horse hangs its head and its eyes are dulled although it will still pick at its hay - but so will a horse with a broken leg! In severe cases of colic the horse will roll on the ground in apparent agony. Modern pain killing drugs, muscle relaxants and laxatives can usually relieve colic. Bill Marshall believes that horses with colic should be kept on their feet for if allowed to roll on the ground the gut could twist and/or strangulate.

CHAPTER THIRTEEN — *The Art & Science of Racehorse Training*

Other Signs

Other danger signs for the onset of the loss of condition are mucus running out of the nose and skin trouble. The racehorse loses its glossy, silky coat which becomes dull and 'leathery' to the touch.

Psychological Factors and Condition

Trainers should ensure that their racehorses are always psychologically content and never over stressed. This applies at all times: in the stable, moving round the yard, running free in the paddock, exercising, jumping and racing. The attention racehorses receive from regular grooming, calm handling, grass nibbling, warming up and down, swimming with a groom in a warm sea etc, is very important in reducing boredom or 'confinement stress' in stabled horses. The more a horse is expertly handled, exercised and given attention the less it is bored: hours of swimming in circles in cold pools or unattended walking attached to mechanical 'roundabouts' can induce stress.

Sudden loss of condition and changes in a horse's behaviour are not due to sudden character changes but are usually due to some physical or psychological reason. The calm, well ordered atmosphere felt in the most successful racing yards is always by design and is one of the great arts of successful racehorse training.

A racehorse must never be humiliated by its work riders or jockeys. Its competitive spirit has to be encouraged and the horse must never be allowed to become bored with the training programme. The horse has to be kept as relaxed and as free from pain as possible during work, but keyed up and 'on its mettle' when about to race.

A sound, well conformed horse in bad condition is often a good buy. To purchase or not becomes a much more difficult decision to make when the horse is well conformed, in bad condition *and* lame. Lameness and its assessment is the subject of the following chapter.

CHAPTER FOURTEEN

Lameness: Assessment and Cure

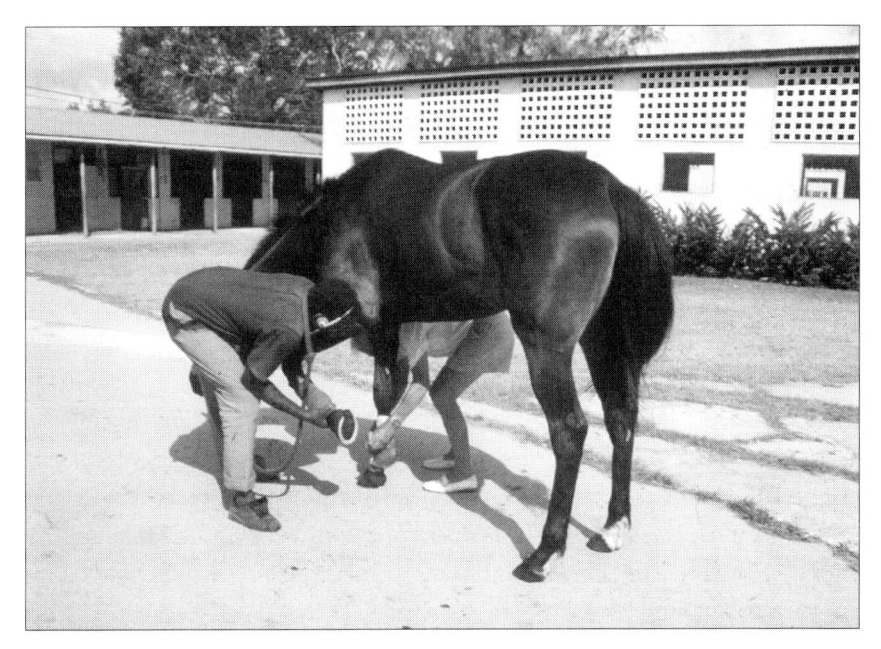

Picking up a leg immobilises the horse for bandaging.

Lameness is any departure from a racehorse's normal gait or action. The pain associated with lameness will affect performance but the pain threshold for lameness is remarkably variable. Some horses will race well despite some low level of lameness but the trainer must understand the original cause of the lameness: some are nothing to worry about, others if not instantly treated, will cripple a horse and end its racing career.

The Search for Lameness

An enormous amount of any trainer's time is spent in examining horses for signs of lameness and any observed changes in the racehorse's gait should result in immediate cessation of the training programme until the cause of the lameness is ascertained and, where necessary, steps taken to bring about a cure.

Lameness is not usually noticeable when an unridden horse is cantering and is best seen when it is walking or trotting. Lameness results in an unevenness in the horse's gait and is often associated with particular movements. In a jumper, pushing off the ground unevenly with its hind legs is often a sign of lameness.

The Trainer's Art

Experienced trainers are constantly running their hands over racehorses legs searching for localised pain, 'heat' and swelling. Lameness can be associated with skeletal damage or 'soft tissue lameness', found for example in tendons, ligaments and muscles. When a soft tissue becomes injured there is inflammation and localised redness and heat. The redness and heat are due to the local small blood vessels, the capillaries and arterioles, expanding (dilating) and increasing local body heat loss. The swelling or inflammation is due to salts, water and soluble proteins escaping from damaged blood vessels and cells into the spaces that surround the damaged tissues. Pain results from nerve endings being activated by the local swelling and from chemical substances that are liberated from the injury sites.

After years of practice trainers become very skilled at finding localised sources of heat or inflammation - especially in the superficial flexor tendon. With their hands they constantly compare one leg with another and experienced trainers are sensitive to the slightest 'flinch' they obtain from the horse they are examining. One of the keys to treating lameness is to locate the trouble spot and to treat it as soon as possible: treatment is often very simple and can involve nothing more than rest for the horse. Hence the greater the skill a trainer has in diagnosing lameness the less likely the horse will break down.

The Science

The diagnosis of the source of skeletal lameness has recently been made more effective by advances in bone scanning, using injected radioactive labels, and radiography. Recent advances in enzyme analysis and ultrasonics have improved source diagnosis for soft tissue lameness. Ultrasound can even be used to help reduce local swelling since, when locally applied, it produces heat. Localised heat will increase local blood flow which will, in the long term, help to reduce swelling.

Often the site of lameness is obvious from a swelling, local pain or heat. Nevertheless the trainer should routinely carry out a *systematic* search for lameness by searching for localised heat and pain. During routine examination the trainer should be on the lookout for common racehorse ailments.

The Box

The racehorse should be first examined at rest and in its box. The trainer should run a hand over the racehorse's back and limbs looking for any swellings, heat, red areas, sensitive spots, cuts and bruises. All the leg joints should be bent to see if this causes any pain to the thoroughbred. Holding the horses leg bent for a few minutes makes some types of lameness more evident if the horse is walked shortly after bending.

The Yard

To search for lameness the groom walks the racehorse up and down on a hard surface with a lead rein that is sufficiently long to allow free movement of the horse's head. A sure sign of lameness is if the horse's stride length is shorter than usual. That is why it is important the trainer examines every horse in the racing stables twice a day in order to know what is 'normal' for each horse.

Turning the horse in circles gives the trainer some idea if there are back problems, especially if there is a change in the gait as the horse turns. After turning the horse in circles the groom is next instructed to run and an almost certain sign of lameness is if the horse 'bobs its head' as it follows the running groom. Head bobbing is often an indication of lameness in the forelimbs. When lameness is severe the head bobs even when the horse walks on a hard surface.

The Canter Track

If work riders regularly ride the same horse, they are quick to spot when lameness is approaching as there is a change in its 'action' during trotting and cantering on the exercise track.

The Neck and Back

A trainer who runs a hand along the horse's back will pick up local pain spots and soreness. There are over 50 vertebrae in a racehorse's back and a common problem in racehorses is vertebral dislocation. This can occur in many different ways - most frequently rolling on the ground when out to grass, jumping and landing badly or during a fast gallop when the horse suddenly hits uneven ground.

A horse with a bad back does not exhibit lameness by 'limping' but its stride or rhythm (its 'action'), is less than perfect. Recognition of imperfect action comes through regular daily observation. A racehorse with a sore back tends to hold itself tensely (as do humans) and this can make matters rapidly worse. A trainer needs to develop a good critical eye for a 'tense horse'.

Many trainers believe that a horse chiropractor is excellent for back disorders. The chiropractor literally 'cracks the racehorse's back' but nowadays there are few horse chiropractors. Bill Marshall believes in its efficacy. In many instances and within minutes of the chiropractor's treatment the racehorse's action was back to normal.

Fistulous Withers

A common back problem is soreness from the saddle pinching or rubbing, which can be avoided by using clean and properly fitting tack. Incorrectly seated saddles can cause an infection of the withers, 'fistulous withers', from bursae which become infected with bacteria. Fistulous withers have to be thoroughly cleaned out with a sterile cloth and disinfected with hydrogen peroxide.

Poll Evil

Infected bursae can give rise to lameness and should always be treated. An infection on the top of the head, 'poll evil', is treated in the same way as fistulous withers by cleaning out and disinfecting. Poll evil develops when there is a bacterial infection of a bursa which is usually formed when the horse strikes its head a hard blow on, for example, low beams. Leather poll caps are useful protection when racehorses travel in cramped conditions.

Forelimbs

Forelimbs, partly because they carry the weight of the jockey, are more prone to lameness than hindlimbs and chip fractures of the small knee bones are quite common in flat racehorses. (There is nowadays an operation that is quite effective for treatment of these chips or 'mice'. A special fibre optic viewing tube, an arthroscope, is introduced into the synovial joint and the chips are removed by microsurgery.)

The horse should stand in a relaxed manner with its front legs parallel. Picking up and resting either of its hind legs on the front of its hooves is normal but if one fore leg is rested in a similar way this is often a sign of lameness - perhaps 'navicular syndrome'.

Navicular Syndrome

In navicular syndrome the navicular bone starts to break up probably as a result of a reduction of the blood flow to the bones. It is rare in young flat racers but can occur in mature jumpers.

Shoulder Lameness

After feeling and examining the back and neck the trainer works down the front of the horse and checks for 'shoulder lameness'. This is limited movement of the shoulder joint and is usually caused by a blow. The cure is complete rest and when the horse starts to improve swimming is a good form of rehabilitating exercise.

Capped Elbows

Forelimbs sometimes develop 'capped elbows' - a soft swelling on the point of the elbow - when, for example, the horse lies down and sleeps on the edge of a shod hoof. A capped elbow is unsightly but causes no harm or pain to the horse and the swelling can be removed by lancing and keeping the horse on its feet, especially while it sleeps.

Elbow Lameness

'Elbow lameness' is as serious as shoulder lameness and is usually associated with a swelling of the elbow joint. The only cure is rest.

Broken Knees

Lameness can be caused by knee wounds or 'broken knees', when the horse stumbles and superficially damages the skin over the knee. If the cut is very deep it has to be stitched and covered with antiseptic ointments. The skin heals from the inside out, so the outside must be kept clean and ointments used to keep infection at bay.

Popped Knees

The trainer should look for 'popped knees'. In this condition the front of the knee has small, soft swellings as a result of damage to the joint capsule. It is not always associated with lameness but if the swelling becomes worse lameness might follow. Rest will help.

Arthritis

Racehorses are prone to arthritis of the knee bones which will cause lameness. This is difficult to detect from a superficial examination, but radiography of the joint will help identify the problem.

Sore Shins

A common forelimb complaint giving rise to lameness in two year olds is 'sore shins' (see pages 120-121) which usually occurs on both legs at the same time. The front of the cannon bones become very sore and the horse shortens its stride. The cure is complete rest for a couple of weeks and a gradual re-introduction into training with gentle exercise.

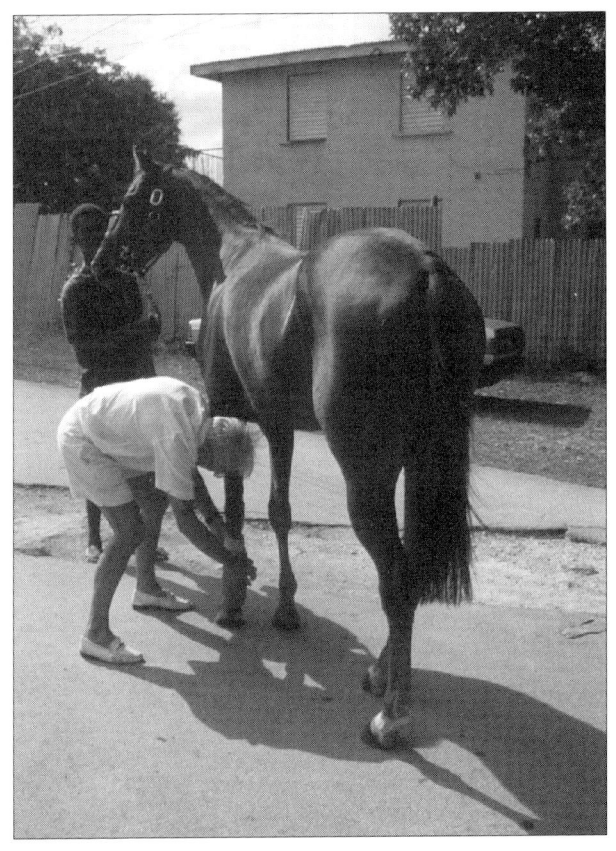

Bandaging is an art.

Brushing and Speedy Cut

Some racehorses have a habit of hitting one leg with another and this causes 'brushing' on the insides of the legs. 'Speedy-cut' is the name given to the cut when it is above the middle of the cannon bone. Horses coming in with speedy cut wounds after work should have their feet carefully checked. Polo bandages wound on both the fore and hind legs help to protect against both of these conditions.

Tendons and Ligaments

The horses tendons are extraordinary long and operate at long distances from their muscles. They are quite exposed and as a result are vulnerable to injury. Tendon and ligament strains, which usually occur in the forelimbs, are some of the most frequent and dangerous causes of lameness in racehorses. Lameness from severe strains or tears to tendons and ligaments can take months or even years to reverse. Thus any sign of a swelling in the region of a tendon has to be treated with caution as serious damage may follow. Unfortunately strains to superficial and deep tendons (superficial digital flexor tendon, deep flexor tendon, see page 38) are not immediately visible and do not, necessarily, cause immediate lameness.

As soon as the trainer detects any slight swelling of the back tendons all work should stop and the racehorse rested in a box. At the site of the swelling a light pressure bandage should be applied over a wad of absorbent cotton material, gamgee, soaked in an anti inflammatory drug like dimethyl sulphoxide (DMSO). Bandaging is a real art and many trainers like to apply leg bandages themselves. If, for example, a pressure bandage is applied too tightly it can cause more damage than the original injury!

The horse can be given pain relieving drugs like phenylbutazone, an anti-inflammatory drug. 'Bute', as it is known, is widley used in racing yards and can be given as a paste in the mouth or as a powder, in the feed or in solution for intravenous injections.

Severely damaged tendons can form 'bowed tendon' when, after the healing process is complete, the tendons and their synovial sheaths (page 37) become deformed by thickening and scar tissue. This is a serious condition and horses with bowed tendons are unlikely to be successful on the racetrack.

Strains to the check and suspensory ligaments (page 50) are treated in the same way as for the back tendons. At the slightest sign of a strain all work must stop. Check ligament strain is seen as a swelling running below the knee, but suspensory ligament strain, which can be anywhere along the length of the ligament, is less obvious. Heat or a swelling on the inside of the limb gives some indication of the site of the strain, and the horse feels pain if any part of this region is touched when its leg is off the ground.

The suspensory ligament splits into two at the bottom of the cannon bone and each half attaches to one of the two sesamoid bones. The bones are attached by ligaments to the pastern bones (see Figure 4.5). If these ligaments are subject to excessive stress and if the suspensory ligament becomes damaged this can lead to *sesamoiditis*. Treatment is the same as swelling to the back tendons, as outlined above.

Pulsating Electromagnetic Field Therapy

Bill Marshall routinely uses pulsating electromagnetic field therapy for treatment of muscle, tendon and ligament lameness and considers its use extremely beneficial for enhancing the general healing process. However, as yet, its exact scientific mode of action is unclear. The muscles are stimulated while the horse is at rest (and racehorses certainly do not appear to object to the treatment) as are the tendon cells by the pulsing electromagnetic fields that are created when electrical current is placed through coils placed on either side of the affected areas. In Marshall's hands some amplitudes and frequencies of signals appear more effective than others in reducing lameness that results from either damaged muscles or ligaments and tendons. There is also some evidence that this type of therapy does improve bone fusion in stress fractures. PEMF for a few hours each day appears to improve the speed at which tendon and ligament strains repair. It is certainly a far less dramatic treatment than 'firing' and 'blistering' tendons and ligaments.

Firing and Blistering

The old idea was that firing and blistering racehorses legs 'stimulated the circulation' at an area of damage and the belief was that the newly induced inflammation would speed repair of the injury site.

At one time 'firing' the legs of lame horses by applying hot irons - in extreme cases sulphuric acid - was used 'to cure' tendon and ligament lameness. It was extremely painful for the horses and they suffered so much that they could not be worked for a year or eighteen months following 'treatment'. Recently, painlessly firing anaesthetised horses by applying heat in lines has been carried out. However there is almost no scientific evidence that firing has any effect on treating any disorder. Similarly for 'blistering' horses legs with substances that cause local inflammation.

Bill Marshall still blisters horses using mercuric iodide but is beginning to doubt the value of the treatment. He always applies the blister to both legs so that the undamaged leg is not subject to undue strain. He believes that firing and blistering appeared to work in some cases in the past, but they were only extremely unpleasant ways of forcing horses to rest!

Splints

Lameness in fore and hindlimbs can also be due to 'splints'. A 'splint' is a term for any increase in size of one of the metacarpals in the forelimb or metatarsal bones of the hindlimb. The splint bones are located on either side of the cannon bone, they give support to the knee bones and they fuse to the cannon bones when a racehorse is four years old. Concussive loading irritates the free ends of the metacarpals and metatarsals and causes splints. Because of this trainers take extreme care with two and three year olds when riding them on hard (road) surfaces. It is also one of the reasons why racehorses should not be jumped before they are four years old.

The most frequent splints are growths between the splint bone and the cannon bone, often resulting in the fusing together of the two bones. Splints only cause lameness if they affect the knee joint. Small splints formed in the upper region of the splint bone develop painfully but once formed, after a few weeks, they are usually harmless. If a horse starts to develop splints Bill Marshall gives it an ounce of dried milk with each of its two daily feeds and cuts back on the amount of work.

Windgalls

Small swellings, 'windgalls', that appear on fore and hindlimbs at the side of the fetlock joint are also not a very serious condition. They can be a warning to the trainer that the horse is working too hard but windgalls do not directly give rise to lameness. The trainer should cover the windgall with gamgee and a pressure bandage and carry on working the horse.

Fetlock Joint

The fetlock joint can become strained and then the joint will swell. If the horse is rested until the swelling has disappeared the lameness will also disappear when the joint is free of pain.

Osselets

'Osselets', round bony outcrops of the sides of the cannon bone at the fetlock joint, sometimes appear in two year olds and there is nothing that can be done to prevent their formation. As soon as they appear they should be covered with a polo bandage stretched lightly over gamgee. Osselets can be painful but as soon as they stop growing they tend not to cause any problems. They decrease in size as the race horse ages.

Ringbone

The pastern bones can cause lameness if they start to grow excess bone, especially if the new growth interferes with the pastern joint. 'High ringbone' is the name of the condition when the growth occurs at the bottom of the long pastern bone or at the top of the short pastern bone. 'Lower ringbone' is a similar condition and happens when bone starts to grow out from the lower end of the short pastern or from the upper end of the pedal bone. Both conditions are probably due to concussive loading, although there is some evidence that the tendency to form ringbones may be inherited.

The racehorse is lame whilst the extra bone is growing and during this period it must not be worked. Bandaging helps and usually once the ringbones are formed the horse can be raced again.

Sidebones

Damage to the cartilage of the pedal bone causes extra bone, 'sidebones', to be produced which results in lameness while the bone is being formed. After the sidebones have formed the racehorse is often sound.

The Feet

The coronet is a sensitive part of the horse's foot and can give rise to a number of problems; nearly all will, but not necessarily, cause lameness.

Tread Wounds

'Tread wounds' may be the result of other horses hitting the coronet region with their hooves or by the horse striking itself when turning. If left untreated a vertical 'quarter line' of improperly formed horn can occur which, if it splits, can give rise to sub-horn bacterial infections.

Quittor

'Quittor' is a discharge from an infection of the coronet often as a result of a tread wound or a puncture wound of the sole and occurs as there is no other site for the discharge.

Sandcracks

'Sandcracks' are vertical cracks in the horn that come down from the coronet. They can be caused by the racehorse being struck on the coronet. If the horse strikes hard ground it can cause 'grasscracks', vertical cracks that lead up from the bottom of the hoof. Surface cracks do not cause any problems but if severe the underlying laminae (see page 49) can become infected. Careful shoeing and even, in some cases, a special resin to 'glue' the crack back together may be needed to prevent on-going lameness.

Hindlimb

Although not as prone to lameness as the forelimb the hindlimb has its own share of special problems. Just as the shoulder joint can become lame so can the hip joint. The cure is, once again, rest. Sometimes the hindlimb will 'seize' due to the locking-up of the stifle joint. There is nothing that can be done and the trainer will have a very lame horse in the yard. If the horse is rested, more often than not, the joint frees off.

Capped Hock

The hock suffers similar problems as the knee (wrist) joint. A 'capped hock' is caused when the hock is struck and a bursa forms. The horse is often lame but usually recovers despite the persistence of a large swelling.

Thoroughpin

Another painless bursal swelling is a 'thoroughpin' - a bursa of the sheath around the deep digital flexor tendon as the sheath and tendon pass down the hock.

Bog Spavin

'Bog spavin' is likewise a painless bursal swelling of the hock joint capsule and often seen on the inside front of the hock.

It is best to leave all these bursal swellings of the hindlimbs alone as they rarely result in lameness and any attempt to suck off the fluid can cause an infection. Infected bursae, such as in fistulous withers and poll evil (see above), can become serious conditions.

Bone Spavin

'Bone spavin' is a form of osteoarthritis of the hock and is a common form of lameness in the horse. It is often seen as the horse comes out of the stable as a stiffness of the hindlimbs which improves with exercise. It appears in jumpers as an unexplained 'loss of heart'. There is sometimes a swelling on the inside of the hock (as a result of an inflamed inner upper end of the hindcannon). The so-called 'spavin test' where the hind leg is bent under the horse for a minute or so (and the lameness becomes worse if the horse is then trotted) is not specific for the hock since the hip and stifle joints are also bent and stressed. There is nothing that the trainer can do for bone spavin except hope that the joint will improve with time.

Curb

'Curb' is another problem linked to the hock and is a ligament strain at the upper edge of the hind cannon which shows up as a bulge. It often occurs when two year olds have been worked too hard on too heavy a ground. Once again the cure is rest. Previously curbs were fired.

Bucked Shins

'Bucked shins' is the hindlimb equivalent to 'sore shins' and is often found in jumpers who consistently hit the tops of fences with their hind cannons. Rest is the cure, along with some soothing lotion such as calamine applied to the shin. Protective boots can be used in persistent offenders.

Muscle Lameness

Horses will frequently strain muscles. If a racehorse is lame and the tendons seem to be in order the trainer should suspect fore or hindlimb muscle lameness. The onset of lameness from strained hindlimb muscles is quicker than from strained hindlimb tendons.

Muscular lameness can be due to direct damage to the muscle fibres (primary muscular lameness) or as a secondary damage to muscle fibres, which is usually brought about by a skeletal injury. Primary lameness is the most common and is sometimes difficult to diagnose as, for example, the racehorse rapidly accommodates its limb action to take into account the damaged muscle fibres.

Two enzymes, Creatine Kinase (CK) and Aspartoamino Transferase (AST), are specific to the inside of muscle fibres. If the blood is analysed for these enzymes and an increase in their concentration found this indicates that there is primarily muscle damage as they are leaking out of damaged muscle fibres.

Tying-Up

Azoturia or 'tying up' is when the muscles of a horse's back and its hindlimbs become painfully stiff and 'seize up' - in extreme cases horses will not be able to move. It occurs in a number of different circumstances but particularly when racehorses are exercised too hard after long periods of rest. CK and AST leak out of the muscle cells and can be detected in the blood. In extreme cases the horse passes dark coloured urine which is contaminated with myoglobin, the molecule that supplies contracting muscles with oxygen. The cure is rest in a box and the administration of muscle relaxants and anti-inflammatory drugs like phenylbutazone. Extra long warming up periods should be used when training racehorses susceptible to 'tying up'.

From the above it can be seen that most cures for lameness are simple and based upon rest in a horse box. Lame horses should not be turned out into the paddock as they may further injure themselves by trying to gallop.

One of the most important fundamental principles of racehorse training is that the earlier lameness is detected, the quicker it is cured. Detection, like so much of racehorse training, is both an art and a science.

Conclusion

Racehorse training requires that a trainer develops patience: patience for muscle, tendon, ligament and bone to grow; patience for the training to assimilate; patience to be, at all times, calm with the horse; patience for choosing the correct race in which to run the horse and, above all, patience to keep the horse fit. Effective training means a trainer is in harmony with the racehorse, learning to work with each horse in the yard and never against it. As a rule horses learn by kindness and a racehorse trainer cannot teach through punishment. Throughout any training programme horses have to be taught. Thoroughbreds may be competitive animals but they are not instinctively racehorses.

The life of a racehorse trainer may seem incredibly glamorous, but much is hard work. In a lifetime Bill Marshall has trained thousands of racehorses - each one slightly different. They have all required dedication. Racehorse training means years of rising early and going to bed late and, besides training racehorses, running and managing a high-risk, complex business. Most people do not realise the amount of work, worry and heartache there is behind every winner. But most trainers would not change their way of life for any other.

Bill Marshall: "Racehorse training is a hard job, but I've also had a lot of fun out of it. Training has given me a rich and wonderful life and one of the reasons I became involved in this book with Michael was to give something back to racing.

Perhaps the hardest thing to learn in racehorse training is that the trainer must never become too close to a horse as at any time, and for any reason, the owner might remove the horse from the trainer's yard. But it is difficult not to become too close, working so intimately with the same horses day after day.

I love my job and, I suppose, a happy trainer makes for happy racehorses. But then it doesn't take a lot to keep me happy - a good yard, a string of horses and, most important of all, I'm out of jail and out of hospital!"

Selected Bibliography

Equine Exercise Physiology (2): Proceedings of the Second International Conference on Equine Physiology. Distributed by ICEEP Publications, PO 1920, Davis, CA 95616. Ed. J R Gillespie and N E Robinson, 1986.

The Classic Racehorse: P Willett. Stanley Paul, 1989.

Horse Racing: D J A Craig. J A Allen, 1982.

Veterinary Notes for Horse Owners: Ed. P D Rossdale. Stanley Paul, 1991.

How Animals Move: J Gray. Cambridge University Press, 1953.

Specifications for Speed in the Racehorse: The Airflow Factors. W R Cook. Russell Meerdink Co Ltd USA, 1989.

Horse Anatomy: P C Goody. J A Allen 1983.

Excerpta Medica International Congress Series No. 87: L D Peachey, 1965.

The Horse's Mind: L Rees. Stanley Paul, 1991.

Horse Structure and Movement: R H Smythe and P C Goody. J A Allen, 1993

Racehorse Training and Sports Medicine: P Swann. Racehorse Sports Medicine and Scientific Conditioning, Australia, 1988.

Index

ACTH, 23
action, imperfect, 166
adrenalin, 22
aerobic conditions, 6
aerobic pathway, 5, 9, 18, 24, 25, 110
airflow, respiratory, 30, 31
al Maktoum, Sheik Mohammed, 80
alveoli, 28, 30
anaemia, 25
anaerobic pathway, 7, 9, 10, 18, 25
antibodies, 53, 54
Archer, Fred, iii
arteries, 25
arthritis, 168, 175
ATP, 3, 4, 6, 7, 8, 9, 10, 12, 19, 22, 25
atrium, left and right, 26
AZT, 176
Babesiosis, 160
bacteria, disease, 53, 54, 73
balance, 45, 89, 90, 91, 149
bars, 49, 87
Berry, Jack, i, ii
bit, rejection, 159
bits
   breaking, 87
   racing, 146
blanket clip, 65
blinkers, 147
blistering, 171, 172
blood typing, 86
body brush, 61
bog spavin, 38, 175
bone
   spavin, 157, 175
   compact, 33
   density, 34, 120
   hardness, 33
   laying down, 119
   long, 33, 34
bones, sesamoid, 170

bran mash, 74
breaking in, 86
Breasley, Arthur, iii, 149
breastplate, 145
British Horseracing Board, 135
broken wind, 85
buffering capacity, 10
bursae, 38, 166, 175
bute, phenylbutazone, 23, 176
Byerley Turk, 82
caecum, 68
calcium phosphate, 33
cannon, conformation, 155
canter, 44
canters, 100
capillaries, 18, 25
carbohydrates, 67, 68, 69
carbon dioxide, 7, 9, 10
cardiac output (CO), 27
cargo planes, 142
carpals, metacarpals, 41, 42, 172
cartilage, 38
cells, animal, 3
centre of gravity, 39, 40, 44, 45, 91
character, 86
check ligament, 49, 50, 170
chiropractor, 166
choking up, 30
CK, 176
clipping
   temperate, 64
   tropics, 65
closed behind, 157
closed in front, 85, 156, 157
colic, 161
collagen, 36, 76
concussive loading, 41, 46
condition, 158, 159
confidence, building, 111
confinement stress, 162

INDEX

conformation, good, bad, acceptable, 85, 154, 155, 156, 157, 158
coronet, 173
cortisone, 23
coughing, 56
cow hocked, 85, 156, 157
CP, 3, 4, 19
cracked heels, 103
cross footed, 158
curb, 175
curry comb, 61
custom feeding, 73
Darley Arabian, 82
diarrhoea, 52
digital flexor tendon, 38
discipline, 92
ditch, 107, 19, 113
DNA, 52
dock, 61
droppings, healthy, 74
dry coat, 77
echocardiography, 85
Eddery, Pat, iv
EIPH, 29
elbows, capped, 167, 168
electrocardiography, 85
encephalins, 23
endorphins, 23
endoscope, 85
entires as jumpers, 108
entries, 133, 134
enzymes, 68
equine influenza, 53
evolved horse's limb, 42
exercise
  bandages, 98
  bits, 87
  tack, 98
  tracks, 100
  severe, 6
  steady, 6
extensor tendon, 38
farrier, 62
fat and fatty acids, 4, 8, 9, 12, 22, 67, 68, 69
fear, trainer's, 93
feed
  store, 57, 58
  race days, 144
  when travelling, 141
feeds, quantity of, 94, 95
feet, conformation, 155
fence
  adjustable, 108, 109, 114, 115
  steeplechase, 109
fetlock, 38, 172
  loads, 47
  conformation, 155

fibre, 71
firing, 171, 172
fitness, 12, 102, 110, 124
  assessment of, 125, 126, 127
  jumpers, 128
  peaking, 130, 131, 132
  sustaining, 130
five digit hand, generalised, 43
flatfooted, 49
flexor tendons, 38, 47, 50
Flying Childers, 83
foot oil, 61
Francome, John, iv
frog, 49, 61, 155
gallop, 44
gallops, 99-102
  half speed, 131
  long and fast, 124
gelding, 117, 118
General Stud Book, 83, 87
girth, 88, 145, 155
glucose, 5
glycogen, 4, 8, 12, 22
Godolphin Arabian, 82
grasscracks, 174
Great Bliss, 96
grooming, 60, 61, 104, 144
grooms, 97
growth hormone, 21
gut, 68
haemoglobin, 24
handicap
  assessment, 137
  races, 134
  system, 136
handicapper, official, 135
hard mouthed, 88
hay, 71, 72
heart
  pump, 25, 26
  rate (HR), 27
  and fitness, 127
  loss of, 128
heat, localised, 164
Hill, William, 54
Hobday operation, 30
hock, 38
  capped, 174
hoof, growth, 62
horse walkers, 98
horsebox, 139, 140, 141, 143
Horserace Betting Levy Board, 136
hurdles, 110, 112, 113
inoculation, 53
isolation/confinement stress, 59, 66
Jarvis, Jack, iv
Jockey Club, 83, 135, 136

INDEX

jumpers
  leading, 135
  novice, 111, 112, 113
  schooling, 111, 112
Keeneland, 80
Kentucky, 80
knee, 38, 155
knees
  broken, 168
  popped, 168
lactic acid, 7, 9, 11, 12, 25, 27
lameness
  elbow, 168
  hindlimb, 174
  muscle, 176
  search for, 163, 164, 165, 166
  shoulder, 167
  tendons and ligaments, 169, 170
large intestine, 68
larynx, voice box, 30, 31, 85
lateral cartilages, 49
ligaments, 35, 38
liver, 68
long rein, 88
loose ring mullen snaffle, 87
lot system, jumpers, 110
lots
  training by, 97, 99, 100, 101, 102, 103
  try outs, 123
lower limb, cannon to hoof, 48
lucerne (alfalfa), 71
lungeing rein, 88
Maloney, Tim, iv
mangers, removable, 73
martingale, Irish, 146
minerals, 70
mitochondria, 5
mucking out, 55, 56, 57, 104
mud fever, 103
Murless, Noel, iv
muscle
  contraction, 3
  excitability, 8
  fatigue, 8
  fibre recruitment, 18
  types, I, IIA, IIB, 15, 16, 17, 18, 20
muscles, flexor, 47
My Swanee, 130
myoglobin, 12, 176
navicular syndrome, 167
neck
  airflow, 30
  conformation, 155
Nelson's Register, 83
Newmarket, 80, 137
nosebands, 146
nostril, 30

nuts, cube feed, 73
O'Brien, Vincent, iv, 80
oats, 68, 72, 73
oestrogen, 23
open
  behind, 157
  in front, 157
osselets, 173
out-bowed, 85, 156
ox-kneed, 158
oxygen, 3, 5, 6, 9, 12, 24, 25, 27, 28
  debt, 11, 12
pace, 149
pancreas, 68
pasterns, 34, 38, 173
pectoral fins/limbs/girdle, 40, 46
pedal bone, 47, 62
pelvic fins/limbs/girdle, 40, 46
PEMF, 171
peptide hormones, 23
phalange, phalanx, 41
pigeon toed 158
Piggott, Lester, iii, 149
plantar cushion, 48
plates, exercise, racing, 63
poll evil, 167
potassium chloride, 75
progesterone, 22
protein, 68, 69
psychology
  of training, 119
  of winning, iv
quittor, 174
racehorses, star, British, 138
races
  Classic, 134, 137
  Cup, 139
  Group, 137
  handicap, 134, 135
Raffingora, 130, 158
rating, official, 136
red cells, 24, 25
reins, draw, 146
respiratory rate, 28
Richards, Sir Gordon, iii
riding out, for and against, 103
rigor mortis, 4
ringbones, 173
RNA, 52, 53
roaring, roarers, 29, 126
Rous, Admiral Henry James, 50, 136
saddle, 88, 145
salivary glands, 68
Salmonella, 52
salts, 75, 164
sandcracks, 174
Sangster, Robert, 80

INDEX

schooling, loose, 111
scrubbing, iii, 151
Scudamore, Peter, iv
shins, bucked, 175
shins, sore, 168
shoeing, 62
sidebones, 173
skeletal muscle, figure, 17
skill factor, 12
skin, 76
sleeping elbow, 62
small intestine, 68
Snaafi Dancer, 80, 84
snaffle bits, 87, 88, 146
sodium chloride, 75
soft mouthed, 87
sole, 49
sore shins, 120
soundness, definition of, 85, 154
speedy cut, 169
spleen, 24
splints, 172
sprinters, 15
    anaerobic training, 124
    assessment of, 122, 120
    conformation, 155
stable
    doors, 55
    lighting, 60
    barn type, 54
    bedding, 55, 60
    box, 55
    lights, 104
    U shaped, 54
    ventilation, 54
    tropical, 59
stay apparatus, 49, 50
stayer, 15, 108
    assessment of, 123
    aerobic training, 124
    conformation, 155
steeplechasers, 114
steroids, 21, 22
stomach, 68
straw, 56
stride length, 120
strike rate, 29
stroke volume (SV), 27
superficial tendon, 38
suspensory ligament, 47, 49, 170
Swannell, David, 136
sweating, 75, 76
swimming, tropical, 95, 96
synovial
    capsule, 35
    joint, 35

tack
    room, 57, 58
    exercise, 59
    racing, 145
tactics, racing, 148, 149, 150, 150
tarsals, metatarsals, 41, 42, 172
Tattersall, Richard, 81
Tattersalls, 81, 83, 84
teeth, 159
temperament, racing, 148
temperature, core, 160
tendon, 3, 35, 36, 37, 119
testosterone, 23
thick winded, 121
thoroughpin, 38, 175
three year olds, jumpers, 108
ticks, 160
Todd, George, iv
toe, fulcrum, 47
trainer/jockey relationship, 147
trainers, unscrupulous, 135
training
    Caribbean, vi
    custom, v
    make or break, v
tread wounds, 174
trot, 44
    collected, 89
    figure of eight, 90
try outs, 121, 122
tying-up, Azoturia, 176
ventricles, 26
vertebrate limb evolution, 40
viruses, disease, 52, 53, 54
vitamins A, B, D, E, K, 70, 72
voicebox, see larynx
walk, 44
warm down, 12, 95, 102, 127
warm up, 10, 95, 176
    tropical, 94
water jump, 109
Weatherby, James, 83
whip, use of, 151
whistlers, 29
white cells, 24, 53
white line, 62
wind certificate, 82
windgalls, 38, 172
Winter, Fred, iv
withers,
    conformation, 155
    fistulous, 166
wood shavings, 56
worms, white and red, 160, 161
yearlings, 79, 80, 81, 83, 84, 86, 90
Zetland, Lord, 154